This book is a must-read if...

- ❖ you have been faced with bias for any reason;

- ❖ you need to find the courage from others of how to break down barriers of discrimination;

- ❖ you feel strongly about diversity and inclusion;

- ❖ you enjoy real-life stories of people beating the odds;

- ❖ you want inspiration from people from different walks of life;

- ❖ you need positive thoughts about belief in yourself and your actions;

- ❖ you want to immerse yourself in journeys of self-discovery;

- ❖ you want to be a change-maker and make a difference to the world around you, whether at home or at work;

- ❖ you want to take inspiration from philanthropist and community champion, Dr Andrea Malam BEM.

What people are saying about Andrea...

"Bias Breakers is one of those rare books that once you start reading, you find yourself drawn into a timeless world. They say that we are hard-wired to learn through stories and, of course, the richer the story, the more we can learn. It is the richness of the stories from the inspiring contributors that makes this book so special. Whether you power through the book in one sitting or choose to read it one story at a time, I know that it will help to inspire and shape so many people."

Kul Mahay
Leadership EQ and Culture Specialist
Public Speaking and Leadership Communications

"The key to change is confronting bias head-on rather than trying to pretend that it does not exist.

Bias Breakers is a well-written anthology from different people, with different backgrounds and experiences narrating their stories on bias breaking and pushing through to create change and be the change they want to see. Their stories have inspired and empowered me to always bring my whole self in everything I do, and to be the best and most confident that I can be, without letting biases dictate who I should be."

Pearl Letlotlo Olesitse
Clinical Research Associate

"This wonderful book contains the stories of women and men who have all challenged bias. Whether the bias were as a result of gender, race, societal expectation, religion, ethnicity or any difference, each story speaks of resilience, courage, strength, tenacity and professional curiosity in using their voice to challenge bias which faced them during their individual journeys.

It is a book where tales of 'transforming pain into power' results in each contributor finding their authentic self instead of accepting societal and/or cultural expectations. I guarantee each story will leave the reader in awe and inspired by their personal stories. They certainly inspired me."

Jackie Malton
Author of _The Real Prime Suspect_ and inspiration for the character DCI Jane Tennison in _Prime Suspect_

"Andrea Malam BEM has captured the mood of today with _Bias Breakers_, her anthology with contributors from all walks of life. She has given a voice to many who were originally unable to tell their own story that will resonate with the reader. Part memoir, part polemic, the stories are wide-ranging, thought-provoking and engaging. Despite many challenges and setbacks, the contributors remain resilient and determined. _Bias Breakers_ is a call to arms, inspiring action for positive change."

Olivia Eisinger
Editor and Proofreader

This book is dedicated to all my co-authors
and those who have faced bias for any reason,
or had the courage to realise
that they want to change that bias.

A collection of stories by those who have
triumphed against the odds

BIAS BREAKERS

BREAKING down
the barriers of discrimination

Courage

Andrea Malam BEM

First published in Great Britain in 2023
by Book Brilliance Publishing
265A Fir Tree Road, Epsom, Surrey, KT17 3LF
+44 (0)20 8641 5090
www.bookbrilliancepublishing.com
admin@bookbrilliancepublishing.com

A CIP catalogue record for this book is available
at the British Library.

ISBN 978-1-913770-66-2

Typeset in Adobe Caslon Pro.
Printed by 4edge Ltd.

Contents

Introduction

We all have scars; we all have stories. Let's share them and empower one another. In this world of being, as you share yourself, you are left with more.

Each one of us has a story to share. Some have more than one.

We live in a diverse society, so biases can affect a wide range of people in different ways. We need to check our own biases and learn from our experiences, as biases can be conscious, unconscious, overt, or covert.

Barriers are there to be smashed down. Barriers that prevent under-represented groups from realising their potential, need to be broken down. We need to be adaptable and resilient at the same time.

Bias breakers are individuals who have experienced or champion injustice in relation to culture, race, age, gender, sexuality, physical impairment, or neurodiversity.

We all need to be the person that builds the bridge through diversity by believing in ourselves and following our dreams. We believe the first steps to true inclusivity are **Awareness** and **Acceptance**.

People need to hear about bias breakers from the leaders who are serving their communities at the most challenging of times.

Thus, this book is a must if you are passionate about influencing cultural and organisational changes that empower others to develop skills and capabilities that drive the best outcomes for themselves and their businesses.

Dr Andrea Malam BEM
March 2023

Don't Stop

by Archna Gohil

"Don't stop because you're tired;
keep going because you're almost there"
Ritu Ghatourey
Indian author

I was born in Kenya as an East African Asian, and came to the UK when I was two years old, so did not really know or remember life in Kenya. I am proud to hear the stories and life experiences from my family. I was brought up in a religious household, where we would hear my grandma sing and pray in the mornings; that was our wake-up call, my siblings and I knew it was time for school.

The early years of my life were all about family gatherings, eating lots of yummy food that Mum cooked, attending religious gatherings at temples, and singing at events (bhajans and garba). We are a singing and dancing family so I was always interested in dancing and socialising. This made me a great networker.

I have always been part of a support group from an early age, being one of five siblings. This meant we all had our household chores, as well as making sure we looked after each other, whether it be at school, Saturday Gujarati classes or Girl Guides. I had a privileged childhood, attending extra activities after school and going on school trips. Summer holidays were spent with my first cousins in Leicester, which we all looked forward to and loved as we helped on their market stall in Northampton. My cousins were like my own brothers and sisters; we would act out scenes from films and pretend we were in a play, or go into our mums' bedrooms and take out their clothes and make a shop on our bed to sell items to each other.

My two best friends at school were Panna and Arti, who were more like my sisters. We lived within five minutes of each other and we would sing when we got together so joined the choir in primary school. There was a time we went back to Panna's house after school and we sang The Bangles' song *Eternal Flame* so loud in the living room, not realising her brother was upstairs! Those were the best days of my life when we sang like no one was watching.

The three of us supported each other in the choir and we even got a chance to sing in a competition in Germany for the school! This was the first time I experienced performing on a big stage. We also performed at the Royal Albert Hall, which was amazing!

Back in school in the 1980s, it was tough growing up in north-west London and being one of the best cross-country runners at school, I was inspired by my fellow running friend; the further she got, the closer I would be behind her. I vividly remember my dad taking me to Bannister Sports Ground in Elstree to train after school and coming out running with me at weekends. I never stopped – perhaps I just don't know how to stop? I just keep going, smashing the challenges that I am faced with.

I broke the normal Asian girl stereotype in secondary school, as I wasn't that interested in studying. I knew I was going places when I made friends from various backgrounds at school and then in the workplace.

My determination comes from my grandma. She suffered a stroke and we took care of her at home, even though she was adamant she didn't need help with anything. Although we were there beside her to support her in the bath, going up and down the stairs, and supporting her to walk with the stick, just in case.

My mum is a strong-minded and giving person who always helped people when we were young, as well as taking care of us all and my grandparents. She used to cook for our neighbours and friends. She brought people together with her tasty food and at any family event we would arrange, everyone wanted Mum's food. Even to this date, none of us can master her famous Gulab Jamun recipe; it just doesn't taste like Mum's!

I learnt at a young age to keep on going...

My parents never pushed me to study or do anything I didn't want to do. I always tried my best at school but it was never good enough to get into university or get a degree. In those days, it was unheard of to drop your studies after school/college and get married at 20.

Just after my second child was born, I began to learn Kathak, a classical Indian dance, which was a challenge at home, work and being a mum. I never gave up, and kept on going till my eldest daughter was five and she started Kathak classes too. I was performing on stage and loving the limelight and dancing.

I was a young mum, living with my in-laws, juggling two children under the age of four and learning Kathak dances, which was not what normal young mums would do. Eventually, I was teaching the beginners classes, kids and adults dance groups, and assisting in organising the annual dance productions, as I was a great networker.

At this stage, I was working in Law Enforcement and assisting staff with diversity issues within the staff group. Being the secretary of the Ethnic Minority Network Support Group had given me a purpose to assist and guide those who weren't able to voice their opinions in the workplace.

There was a time I supported a colleague who was on long-term sick leave owing to how she was treated within her department. I would go and do welfare visits to her once a week to make sure she was okay. This wasn't a part of my role but as the secretary of the staff group, we had been tasked to assist her case at tribunal and make sure she was given the correct support from the organisation. I organised network events for staff members so they felt included within the department/unit they worked for.

My colleagues and I would make sure boundaries were set between management and staff to ensure the diverse workforce were always given opportunities for training and to liaise with the policy and procedures departments to assist with policies that affected our staff group members.

It was a demanding role outside of my normal day-to-day job within the organisation. This gave me a sense of achievement at the end of the day, knowing I had made a difference to someone's work-life balance or just peace of mind when they got home. But sometimes I would get home and still be thinking about work or dance routines.

Looking back at that chapter of my life, I have embraced the challenges every step of the way and handled it the best way I know. I decided to divorce my husband and leave my two girls with their father and their grandmother. I felt this allowed them to stay in a safe, stable place that they called home. Home is family and is important to us all; a safe place where you can be surrounded by love. I tried to move forward with a smile and not a care about what people would think or say about me.

It was a difficult time for my family to digest the outcome of my decisions. The challenges of being there for my children whenever they needed me, as well as starting all over again to look for a place of my own so they could spend more time with me.

Both my girls have had privileged childhoods as they go on holidays with their dad and come stay with me, as well as going away for school trips and with the Scouts. Divorce isn't easy for anyone, but whatever challenge I faced, I dealt with and kept on going as I knew I had more work to do.

I remember the time I was at my brother's wedding in Goa and my girls couldn't attend with me. This was probably the worst situation I was faced with, surrounded by my family, having to explain why my children were not with me and being happy for my brother's big day. From that trip to India, I realised I was always going to be alone on this journey, although I had a big family who was always there to support me.

Things got better as time went by; time is a great healer, as they say. My turning point was when I hit 40, and I knew I could achieve more. I started running again to keep fit; whilst I was running, it made me feel like I was 18 again, I could achieve anything! Network marketing and self-development is what I focused on at this stage of my life. As well as volunteering at CRC London, I was a volunteer usher at the church and helped with events and networked with like-minded people.

Being a part of something that is bigger than just living life for yourself was not what I was destined to do; I had a lot of faith in what I was doing and being the humble servant.

Therefore, I tell you, whatever you ask for in prayer, believe that you have received it, and it will be yours. (Mark 11:24)

The Bible started making more and more sense to me, and I started praying for a better future with my children and my career, and meeting the right kind of people to share my life with. I was recognised as the social one, there to help yet always talking to people and being curious to know more about them.

This led me to a change of career back into HR/ Recruitment, which I loved doing at the British Transport Police (BTP).

I helped set up the first Ethnic Minority Staff Group which I was a part of from the launch in 1996.

Last year, I attended a reunion for the BTP after 25 years. It was amazing to see so many familiar faces again and that everyone remembered me as the young friendly-faced girl in HR! I had made officers smile every time they had an issue with sickness, uniforms, or anything HR related.

My time in Law Enforcement and being involved with staff groups was a great sense of achievement for an Asian female who had two children and was divorced. I broke barriers that came my way and faced the challenges, as well as keeping myself busy networking, meeting new people, motivating and cheering them on, and finding ways to help other women who were facing similar challenges in their lives.

I have had many changes in my career and personal life including working in sales, in a 20-to-30-year-olds' environment, helping to break that age barrier. Being one of the eldest in the team didn't stop me from becoming one of the top sellers and then on to helping train sales staff to be the best.

I feel proud about this, considering that when I started in this company, I thought, "They all seem very young and full of energy; how am I ever going to compete with them?" It wasn't about being in competition with young colleagues of mine, it was a challenge in doing my best and showing them age does not make a difference if you are good at the job you are doing.

When I left due to relocating to London, the CEO messaged me and asked me to come back if my circumstances changed.

This is a company with over 400 employees, and different departments with various skill sets, and yet he still asked me to come back within the sales team.

Then I worked for a company in London, which had little or no respect for staff and colleagues, where I was often referred to as "Little Person". But I'm not little in age or little in height, so whom did they mean? I stated, "I have a name – it's Archna!" It was ignored, and I was made to feel worthless. There was no way I was taking this, coming this far in my life, and being disrespected in this way, so I left after a couple of months.

After assisting and fighting for ethnic minority colleagues within the police force, I felt even more passionately and strongly that I had to bring my journey to others.

After meeting that special person and relocating to North London, and being a volunteer, I am now working for Next Steps, a supported living recruitment company, and giving back to support people with autism and learning disabilities. I believe this is my purpose; speaking to people, getting to know them and being curious is what I love doing.

I would like to think I have made a difference to everyone that I meet. Recently a colleague of mine thanked me for encouraging him to do better and think bigger than what he thought he was capable of and thinking about a career change. I supported him through a time when he felt he was not reaching his potential and reminded him what he could bring to others. I encouraged him to make the change in his career which was a great move for him.

Within a week of starting at Next Steps, I felt like I was a part of the family and had been there for years. My boss kept on saying to me, "Where have you been hiding all these years?!" My passion for people shines through in the work I do, thinking out of the box to find solutions and encouraging people around me.

My partner always says, "You can't sit still and have ants in your pants!" which is right! I am a go-getter and will speak my mind when necessary, especially when it comes to someone being treated unfairly and not being heard. I have seen this happen many times in my career and personal life.

My daughters know I speak my mind and sometimes say too much, but this is me! The experiences I have encountered and the stereotypical barriers I have broken, have made me a stronger person to keep challenging myself and keep going. Now that both of my girls are at university making memories of their own, my legacy to them would be to be yourself; face challenges head-on like it's just another day and it will pass; never change for anyone; be respectful and humble in what you say or do in life; and to surround yourself with like-minded souls who uplift you and bring the best out of you.

If we try to think out of the box and challenge the status quo, then we are all bias breakers.

Special

by Louise Slattery

I am an incredibly proud mother to a "special" autistic child, Kieran. This is not a sentence I ever thought I would say! Then again, would any mother expect to have a child with autism?

Not only am I the mother of an autistic child, but to two more children, Danny and Sunny. I am extremely lucky to have three sons, when I once couldn't even dream of having just one. My husband and I tried and failed to conceive naturally. I had a burning desire to become a mother that took over my entire existence. I remember at that time looking around and all I could see were either pregnant women or people with children.

When we married, people kept assuming that we were just enjoying our freedom. I couldn't bear to tell people that it wasn't happening. I felt a deep shame that the most natural thing in the world wasn't as natural as one once thought. My brother and his girlfriend got pregnant at this time too. I was devastated that they managed it, yet I couldn't. I clearly remember buying them a Babygro for their baby for Christmas. I sat on the floor in my flat wrapping it, I held it in my arms and hot tears rolled down my face, the crying that you didn't expect nor couldn't stop. My heart literally felt like it was breaking into a million drops of tears.

We finally spoke to doctors and after some tests, we found out I had polycystic ovary syndrome (PCOS). The fertility specialists were so lovely. They decided to operate on my ovaries; this was a keyhole surgery and didn't hurt as much as I expected. The aim was to drill holes into the ovaries which could reverse the condition and even make fertility treatment more effective afterwards, but we still didn't conceive.

In the end, we went back for fertility treatment. We had to go for daily scans while taking medicine (Clomid) that would technically grow the eggs to ensure we could then be able to fertilise naturally. We would literally be told when to go home and 'have the D' which never felt romantic, and afterwards, my legs would be up in the air for at least half an hour tightly closed and fingers crossed. Each month ended with a single line on a test. I can't even count how many negative tests I have peed on. It was a heartbreaking time, to say the least!

We were on our last try before they were going to move us onto IVF. Suddenly my husband's mother got ill in Nepal, and he had to fly home. Unfortunately, his mother died before he arrived. It was such a sad time all round. A few weeks after he returned, I started to feel weird… was I pregnant? He had only been back for a few weeks so it was very unlikely. I peed on yet another test and to my utter shock, it was positive! I can't even express how I felt, apart from being the luckiest person in the world. My husband's face was a picture of pure happiness, tears welled up in his eyes. It's a memory I will never forget.

A few weeks later, I had a blackout and was taken for an emergency scan to check if the baby was okay. It was then we found out I was not a few weeks pregnant, but I was pregnant before my husband even left. The last round of Clomid had been a success!

I thought a lot about fertility treatment and possible links to autism. At my second scan, they also found an issue with the baby's umbilical cord, something called a single-vessel cord. They had to check the baby with growth scans but he grew well and had no other issues. This was also something I thought about in the future.

Unbelievably, my next two sons were conceived naturally and we never had any issues during pregnancy. Neither of them has autism.

At first, it was incredibly hard for us as parents to notice the early signs of having an autistic child. As a baby, he did not sleep well, and he still doesn't. He would never settle and would cry for long periods of time. He could not be swaddled as he didn't like his arms trapped and he would never, ever, self-soothe. I read a lot of baby books to try different things. Nothing we tried worked. We once tried the "crying it out" method. I wouldn't recommend it – ever!

The one thing he did like was motion. I could put him into a pram and, like magic, he was asleep. But as soon as those wheels stopped, his eyes popped open. I can safely say I walked miles in those early years. This did wonders for my baby weight loss, though I now can see why things didn't work.

Hindsight is a beautiful thing. At that precious time, I just felt like I was failing at motherhood. It's a crazy thing that when we have children, we put huge conditions on ourselves to be the perfect mother in the world. I realise that the new age society painted a picture of perfect motherhood that I was unconsciously measuring myself against. If I could go back in time and tell myself something, it would be along these lines:

"All families are different, and we don't need to be perfect, just loving!"

I did hear one quote around that time which helped. "Nothing stays the same forever, it will pass." I always remember this when having a bad day, even now. I also repeat this a lot to my clients in my hypnotherapy practice to this day.

When my son was waking at two-hour intervals, my sleep-deprived brain would mutter these words of optimism, and nothing did remain the same forever.

The main issue we had in the early years was huge attachment anxiety. He would always want to be with me or my husband. The only others he would talk to was his nanny and grandad. This is still an issue now. Back then, if a stranger looked at him, he would cry and when he was a toddler, he would hide. He has had a blanket since he was a baby; he thought no one could see him if he put it over his head. I think he thought he had a magic invisibility power! At the time of writing, he is still taking the blanket everywhere. Once we lost it when it fell on the ground on the walk to school. The anxiety was real, for us mainly. Someone had put it next to a bin, but thank God it wasn't taken by the bin men! He also had a teddy dog (still to this day) which he took everywhere. He named it Missy. He called her his best friend when he was small because he couldn't make friends. This dog must be 100 years old because he decided she had to have a birthday with a cake every few weeks…!

The thing I didn't notice for years was he didn't look anyone else in the eyes, just us. He also did not respond to us if we did not use his name. For instance, if I walked into the room and asked, "Do you want a drink?" he wouldn't respond. I had to be very specific that I was talking to him, and ask, "Kieran, do you want a drink?" His communication was different. Even though he knew how to speak, he often selectively chose not to, and never, ever to strangers.

When Kieran was a toddler, he used to point at what he wanted and make grunting noises. This was annoying, to say the least! Even now he still makes noises but mainly when angry. However, I am very grateful that he can speak, because this is not the case for some children on the spectrum. He does struggle with the pronunciation of words; he can't say the letter S very well and can sound like Jonathan Ross. He once said "fidget spinner" in such a funny way that I couldn't help but wet myself laughing. Most of the time, I ignore it, as he is having speech and language sessions with a specialist. I did try to help him with this, but he got so upset and frustrated with himself.

The hardest part was when we decided to send him to nursery at two years old. This is when we realised how bad his attachment was. He wouldn't let me leave the room and the teacher had to drag him off me daily while he was literally kicking and screaming. As a parent, this was heartbreaking, so I turned into a mummy spy, looking through the window of the nursery class. (I was allowed to do this, by the way!!) It was only three days a week, but he was still having naps and they couldn't get him to sleep. He looked exhausted and upset when I would pick him up and extremely happy to be back home. At school, he also wouldn't eat; eating was, and continues to be, an issue.

This was when I realised there was something different about him. His behaviour started to get worse. He would have terrible temper tantrums over seemingly simple things. He once had a meltdown because I cleaned up his mess; he wanted it back, exactly as it was!

I clearly remember saying to my mother that I thought something was different about him. She didn't believe me. I was often told that Kieran was just a naughty boy, who needed better discipline. A lot of the older generation would say Kieran needed to be slapped! I do not agree with hitting children! My husband echoed that he was naughty, and he didn't think anything was wrong.

Personally, I believe that there is **no such thing as a naughty child**; there always seems to be a reason behind it, medically or background and environment.

At this point, I yet again felt like a failing mother. I was my own worst enemy. Was I too soft on him? Maybe it was all my fault... I wish I followed my motherly instinct sooner. I believe a motherly instinct is the strongest instinct you will ever have and many of us do not follow this. The problem was that I knew he was different but at the same time, I didn't want him to be. I was fighting between my head wanting the perfect child that one expects, and my heart screaming that this was not who Kieran was. It took until he was five to finally get a diagnosis...

When Kieran started school, his condition blew up in our faces like an explosion of TNT. Apparently, this is a common time for the condition to gain momentum. Previously, his days had consisted of play-focused learning. When he started school, he did not enjoy sitting and concentrating on the work in a structured way which is not enjoyed by many autistic children. His way of expressing this was through his behaviour.

He started having daily meltdown battles at home which could continue for hours. His meltdowns were getting very violent and he was getting bigger and stronger. He would lash out at anyone and seemed to never care about anyone's feelings except his own.

One day he wanted to watch a programme on TV, but couldn't because it wasn't on that day. He started yelling, "I want it!" followed by grunting sounds. This continued for about half an hour. Repeating the sentence and sounds, over and over and over. There is no reasoning with him at this point when he has gone into "meltdown world". He then tried to kick and punch his brothers. I picked him up and put him in his room to calm down.

What he did next was try to destroy anything in his path like a tornado. Picking up anything and throwing it at the walls of his room – as a consequence, his bedroom wall is full of dents and chips. He was destroying not only his toys, but also his brothers' toys! He was screaming in a complete rage and crying at the same time. At this point, I knew better than to talk to him until his anger has calmed down. Finally, he tried to break his bedroom window so I had to try to control him.

I tried to hold him, but he started to kick me, then punched me so hard that I passed out. I was fine but my husband said he didn't seem to care even then about hurting me. This meltdown lasted nearly two hours.

These were happening daily, and whenever we tried to find out why, Kieran would simply shut down. He couldn't express his emotions – and still has issues now. It was an awful time for me to watch my baby boy being so angry and upset, knowing he couldn't even help it.

At school, his teacher was also having problems with him not cooperating or joining in with any activities, and he still didn't have any friends. One day when picking Kieran up, I asked his teacher how he had been that day. Her response was totally unexpected and will be engraved in my memory for life…

"Never in all my years working with children have I ever seen a child like Kieran."

I was flabbergasted at her response! I turned to her and responded in the proudest motherly voice, "That's because he is SPECIAL," and walked out of the class with my special son.

Kieran was struggling to manage in school and never wanted to go. We had to deal with daily violence and watch him suffer while we dragged him to school. One day I decided to ask the school to have a look into Kieran's behaviour. I wrongly thought I would be given the help I needed.

Instead, my husband and I were subject to scrutiny as parents. The deputy headteacher decided that Kieran must have been struggling with something at home. I understood why parents must be questioned; however, Kieran's behaviour was the same at home as it was at school.

I felt completely attacked as a mother. I didn't know a thing at the time about AUTISM.

The deputy head recommended parenting courses which I felt appalled at. I still felt something was wrong and I wasn't being heard. One day I picked him up from school and Kieran was crying. I asked him why and he said the headteacher had taken him into her office all day, asking about our home life. Did anyone hurt him at home?

I called a meeting with them and went a little crazy, if I'm honest. I was hurting not only because Kieran was suffering at school, but also because I had to defend myself at the same time. I told them I wanted to move Kieran to a new school.

The very next day, I had to pick Kieran up again after only one hour in school. He destroyed the school classroom and they had to move all the children out for their safety. Therefore, they could no longer have him in a class and isolated him for the whole next year. He had to work in a tent in the hall after that day with no other children.

Finally, after a lot of struggles, I was called into a meeting where they told me they had a school willing to take my NAUGHTY child. I was pleased as I knew Kieran needed a new setting. I was told the school could help Kieran and dealt with children with special needs.

One day by chance, a family health visitor came around to visit us and asked about Kieran's schooling. When I gave her the name of the school, she was shocked! She told me not to send him to that school. She had worked there and knew that this school did not cater for kids with special needs but was a last resort when children had been kicked out of schools with other behaviour issues, not related to special needs.

I was so upset that the school LIED to me.

I called the deputy head and told her that I was not sending him to the school she had suggested. She said that she couldn't keep him as she didn't have the resources. She gloated that the only way would be a one-to-one teacher, which the government would not pay for. I told her that the government would have to, otherwise, I would be taking him out of school.

I took him out of school that very day. The council came around and politely informed me to send him back or I would be breaking the law and I could be prosecuted – what a cheek! I informed them that they were breaking the duty of care law by not having a placement for my son that was fit for purpose.

I won the battle and got a one-to-one teacher for Kieran. I would like to say I was grown up and mature but I swaggered into the school smiling at the deputy head teacher and boasted, "I thought you said they wouldn't pay!"

My little victory was short-lived, as a few days later Kieran came home and told me something that broke my heart into a thousand pieces.

"I wish I was DEAD!!" He looked me coldly in the eyes and meant every word. I am welling up now even as I write. How on earth could a six-year-old child be so depressed to no longer want to be alive?

Although this was the worst moment, it also became the best.

I turned into the 'super mummy' who needed to fix my child. I was no longer messing about with the school. I instantly called our GP who was the most helpful person in the world. She referred me instantly to a mental health team.

When we had our first meeting with our mental health team, they knew instantly Kieran had autism, although he still needed to be assessed, which takes about a year. I was shocked when I heard the word – I didn't know a thing about it, apart from what I had seen in films. (Yes, *Rain Man* with Dustin Hoffman and Tom Cruise.)

I sat for a LONG time and contemplated her words. I had been looking at a complicated puzzle with pieces missing all this time and finally, the complete picture came to life before my very eyes. It finally set us free.

When the school got the report from the mental health team, their attitude improved dramatically and they started to help Kieran at last. But the best thing was that the deputy headteacher left, in a cloud of smoke. I heard rumours that she was getting sacked.

From the moment we got the report, I never had to deal with her again, although before she left, she referred us to Social Services. They couldn't believe they had been called and instantly dropped Kieran from their records. I couldn't tell you how much her final act upset me; I don't think I could put it into words.

It did make me wonder how many families and children had been labelled BAD, when actually they had problems that weren't diagnosed or uncovered. I feel that a lot of autistic children from less fortunate backgrounds would be completely failed by the system and labelled naughty. It's a frightening thought.

How many children with special needs have been let down, in the UK, Europe and developing countries?

How many parents can't fight like me because English isn't their first language?

How many parents have been punished?

How many children have been punished?

How many children believe they are NAUGHTY?

NOT all disabilities are visible!

In the years that followed, the extent of school neglect became so apparent. Kieran felt like he was naughty for so long, when he wasn't. When I told him his diagnosis, his first words were… "So I am not naughty, Mummy?"

We continue to struggle with bias every day. Recently we queued for the disabled toilet and the security guard told us to join the other queue as he could not see that Kieran was disabled. I told him, "He is autistic," to which I heard back, "Well, he doesn't look it." I can't even tell you how many times this has happened and will continue to happen. Along with my personal favourite, "Oh, they didn't have autism and ADHD in my day, only naughty children." It makes my blood boil!

We should always stop and think before we judge, before we make assumptions. That no matter how a person 'looks', things are not always what they seem. I hope that by reading this chapter, the next time you are about to judge a child, a parent or a type of behaviour, take a minute to just remind yourself that NOT all disabilities are visible.

Maybe that child annoyingly kicking your seat on the bus is not naughty. He might be trying to control his emotions. Maybe that child screaming in the supermarket for something is not spoilt. She might be having an emotional regulation meltdown. Maybe that mother who can't seem to stop her child from misbehaving is not a bad mother who doesn't discipline her child… she is trying her darn best! And just maybe, instead of judging, at that moment you could ask if they need any help.

KINDNESS really means the world to a struggling parent with a special needs child, diagnosed or not, believe me.

I wonder how many times you can remember yourself judging a situation? I truly hope that you will in future remember these words. NOT all disabilities are visible.

I am pleased to tell you that Super Mummy finally got Kieran a place in a specialist setting. This took two years and another legal fight! But the day he started at the autism school, he was like a different child. He was happy and smiling and even spoke to new people. It was a long journey that I would never want to repeat, but in the end, Kieran got what he needed.

Previously to having a child with a disability, I thought that disabled people would get all the help they needed when they needed it; oh, how I was so naive! You must be prepared to fight and fight, and fight some more, to get what you need for your child. I will continue to fight all my life to change the BIAS around invisible disabilities and I hope you will join me with a simple change of perspective.

"Recognizing and respecting differences in others and treating everyone like you want them to treat you, will help make our world a better place for everyone."

Kim Peek, American Savant, who was the inspiration for the character of Raymond in the 1988 film, Rain Man.

Dedicated to my first love, Kieran Bajracharya.

I have a dream!

by Nirmala Bhojani

I was born in New Delhi, the capital of India, but grew up in Pune (also known as the Oxford of the East), moving there with my family when I was five years old.

I know I had a wonderful childhood, with flying lessons at 17, unlike most of the kids I knew! We all learned to ride bikes and scooters, and drive cars, but it was very rare to meet girls who learned to fly in the seventies.

I know it was a privilege that my father worked as an aeronautical engineer at the School of Flying in Pune, so I got the same opportunities as my two younger brothers.

My parents were both highly educated in post-partition India, so they had no stereotypical Rules for Girls! My friends would tell me how they weren't allowed to do things which were "for boys". I would laugh and say, " Why?"

Some would share stories about how strict their dad was, but I was glad my dad wasn't like that. I was blessed to have a dad and mum who never said "Girls can't…" to me. So, when I was growing up, I thought I could be anything I wanted to be!

I became a journalist at 20, with the opportunity to interview the late Prime Minister Indira Gandhi, as well as writing a youth column for the local newspaper. Seeing my first byline, my name in print as I wrote for newspapers and magazines, gave me a thrill, far greater than flying ever did! I felt like people were reading the stories and articles I wrote, so I was a part of their daily lives, as most of us had the newspapers delivered every morning in those days.

When I got married, life changed suddenly as I flew to Malawi in East Africa. What a culture shock it was for me, from being a 21-year-old who felt the world was my oyster, to realising that being a woman was a disadvantage, a curse, some form of bad luck!

I had arrived in Blantyre, Malawi to join my husband's extended family, including my in-laws, their three daughters, their other son and his wife.

I was told, "A good wife must not show her teeth, talk or laugh loudly, or look at men," and a whole lot of other nonsense from the dark ages. Along with the old-fashioned values came the abusive and aggressive behaviour of the man who professed to love me, who had come to India with his mother, asking for my hand in marriage.

Little did I know when I accepted what I was letting myself in for! Marrying into a family which was a stark contrast to my own, I was shocked to see that men sat at the table to eat, served by the women, who then ate after they cleared the table.

But I knew I had chosen this marriage, so I felt like it was my fault, that I could not burden my parents with my misery.

So, I kept quiet.

Becoming a mother at 23 was another life-changing situation and having none of my maternal family to support me, I sought advice from the females in the family. They were always happy to give me advice, which was often the same things they had been brought up with: sexist conditioning on how to conform to social norms in the dark ages.

The responsibility of motherhood lay entirely on my young shoulders, and I must be not just a good wife, daughter-in-law and sister-in-law, but also a good mother now...

I had started helping in the shop they owned, as there wasn't much a woman could do then, except cook, clean and shop. How I wanted to leave and return to my parents, who had no such issues, and be just their daughter again. So, I decided to go back home. Home to have my dad comfort my baby as he rocked her when she cried all night. To have my mum make me nourishing food, and to have the maid give my exhausted body a massage, as I was worn out by a long labour and delivering a new life.

But my respite was short-lived as the baby's father arrived. He begged and pleaded that I give him another chance, so I believed him and returned with the six-month-old baby.

A leopard can't change his spots – I had heard the cliché but now I knew it was true.

When my daughter was four years old, we flew out from Blantyre to London for the wedding of one of my younger sisters-in-law, along with the rest of the family. My in-laws decided we should settle in the UK, so we rented a place in South Harrow, and they went back to wind up the shop, when I discovered I was pregnant with my second child.

It was 1986; the coldest winter in 80 years, they said. Inches of snow covered the ground as I wondered what sins I had committed in my last birth to deserve this! Being brought up in the Hindu faith, I thought it must be karma from my past birth, as I had never done anything wrong in this one. Having a strong spiritual family, and believing in humanitarian values of compassion and selfless service as taught by the great Guru Nanak, I felt I had been kind and honest.

Yet, I had landed in the coldest winter, in a new country, to give birth to a new baby, with no mother to help me this time. Having found a weekly newspaper in London to write for (ironically called *New Life*), I started writing a woman's column.

My inner creative joy knew no bounds. At last, I felt like I had a voice again. But with a five-year-old daughter, who had just started school, and a newborn, it was difficult to get to places on the London Underground.

Pushing the little one in a buggy, I would drop my older daughter off at school and head off to find the people I needed to interview for my stories. No maternity leave or anything, I was a journalist, working with my baby who accompanied me, sleeping through most of my interviews, as she adjusted to a world where we got around on the Tube!

When my baby turned one, my in-laws decided to move to Leicester and it was the most multicultural city that I had ever seen. It was more Indian than India, I thought when I saw the miles of saree shops and takeaways in the Belgrave area of Leicester. They bought a house here and I got a part-time job at Dixons so I would drop my older child at school and go to work. Another year of misery followed, and I decided to head back home.

History repeated itself as again, my ex followed me to India, begged me to return and promised to change! Like most young mums, I believed him and came back to Leicester, which had now become home as I made friends and found a job with the library services and the local newspaper.

I decided I could no longer live with my husband and his family so I left. Leaving the marital home, with just a suitcase and my two girls, was the best decision I have ever made. When I heard my ex say, "You will never survive without me!" I thought, "Just you watch me!"

Renting a place, and buying everything we needed, I built a home for my daughters and even had a spare room where friends could come to stay when they were going through tough times. Within five years, I managed to buy my own house, with help from my parents who gave me money for the deposit.

I was so independent that initially, I was not willing to accept help from my parents but when my father came over to visit, he said, "I would rather give you your inheritance while I am alive, to see you in your own home, than after

I am dead." He passed away suddenly after they flew back home and I was heartbroken, but after returning from a visit to mourn with my mother, I started looking for a place to buy.

Being near the girls' school was a priority, so I found a place nearby and after my offer was accepted, I found a builder who renovated the property and did all I wanted to make it my dream home.

In the early days when I was working, I realised that many mums could not work as they needed to pick up the kids from school, so I started campaigning for after-school clubs in the nineties, along with other mums, and we organised a petition with over 2,500 signatures to hand over to Leicester City Council, which was followed by funding for primary schools to start the after-school clubs. Mums could work now till five o'clock and pick up the kids after they finished. A small step in helping women towards financial independence, it gave women a chance to achieve their dreams too.

Setting up a support group for victims of domestic violence and abuse was my next dream, so when two local primary schools asked me if I wanted to do it as they had funding, I jumped at the opportunity to help other mothers. In the new millennium, the local council offered funding to set up community projects, and with two friends I set up Empowering Women to Win, a project in the Belgrave area of Leicester. Many women had arrived in this area with hardly any education and we trained about 250 women to find work through courses, careers advice and mentoring.

Breaking biases in a city like Leicester, where most people worked in the hosiery or food industry, where women were mostly seen and not heard, I guess I was a rare breed; a single mother, journalist and community activist with a voice I raised at every injustice.

Financially independent, I worked three jobs to pay off my mortgage and when my younger daughter qualified as a teacher and said, "Mum, you can stop working now, I can pay the bills," I jumped at the opportunity to travel and see the world as I had always dreamed.

So, at 52, I gave up my work and set off to explore the world, fulfilling another dream. Before I set off, I was offered the chance to publish my first book of true stories called *Ordinary Women, Extraordinary Lives* by the Asian Foundation of Philanthropy and I jumped at it.

I interviewed eight wonderful women in Leicester who had overcome challenges to do whatever they wanted, and I was truly inspired by them!

Travelling in Koh Samui, a beautiful island in Thailand, I would sit on a balcony overlooking the sea, editing the stories for the publisher, so the book was ready to launch in the International Women's Month of March that year.

In 2008, I had my first grandchild, who was diagnosed with autism, so I became a carer to help support families who had children with special needs and disabilities. With a passion to help both my own family and others who were in the same boat, I started campaigning for them, as well as others who were marginalised due to their circumstances.

The Covid lockdown brought other issues, such as a rise in domestic violence, mental health and anxiety issues, so getting together a team of volunteers from all over the world, I set up the campaign to #bethechange on the WOW Woman of the World Facebook page (more details on WOW on page 140). With a team of over 30 volunteers, we offer support to women all over the world who have suffered from domestic violence and abuse.

In 2017, I founded the WOW Women of the World Awards to honour those who make the world a better place and raise funds for a charity called Healing Little Hearts, which performs life-saving operations for children born with heart problems in poorer countries. The Awards gave me the opportunity to meet some amazing people, who truly deserved to be honoured, and we carried on, even through the pandemic.

I feel blessed to have had some great friends and supporters who have believed in me, held my hand, and walked beside me through some dark times. There are too many to name, but I know that we grow together when we help each other!

My motto is:

"Hold fast to dreams, for if dreams die
life is a broken-winged bird that cannot fly!"

Langston Hughes
American poet, social activist, novelist, playwright,
and columnist

Flames of Resistance

by Jermaine Gregory

Growing up in Handsworth, Birmingham in the early nineties, I was fairly guarded by my mother. I wasn't out late in my early teens, as some of my friends were who lived more locally to school. I lived too far away to be out late. So football in the park after school wasn't a thing for me, other than the one time I stayed out (without telling my mother), playing football with a classmate and someone from two years above they knew, and a bunch of others they knew.

As I look back now, I consider how this is a glaring disparity that has been a resonating theme throughout my life and for many others. The theme of how the impact that is felt by those who have to travel further to get to a place of study or work, influences their results. Beginning with children and young people, typically from families and backgrounds that are not particularly well-off, or in areas that are mismanaged in regard to local council financing and provision of needs considered as oversubscribed for budgeting. We can talk about that another time. Though the inherent choice made to participate in this endless capitalist experiment model under the guise of comfort in this country, leaves much to be desired for me. The irony, I tell you, never leaves me.

My family moved from Handsworth to Balsall Heath as I started high school so I then had to get two buses to school. Earlier starts led to the odd later finishes as I participated in extracurricular activities, especially playing football for the school. These late finishes depended on which school we were coming back from; we might get dropped a short walk from our door, or back at school and have to make the trip home at a time when we would catch the tail of the rush hour, along with what seemed like irregular bus scheduling.

This lifestyle and the impact commuting time has on those who live more than 20 minutes away has knock-on effects over time. This, as did the fears around the kind of lifestyle that was permeating the area on the back of the notable moments of the Handsworth Riots in the late seventies, early eighties, nineties and then again in 2011 – the year before London hosted the Olympics – adds further stress on parents and children relationships. If you're a parent with underlying worries about your child, those feelings can present in ways that can hinder your child's growth as you move to protect them from the thoughts in your own mind.

(After mentioning the riots back in 2011, a notable moment which seemed to light the spark for what ensued, I wanted to honour those who have passed due to being a victim of a system using bias, prejudice and power to end life.

We won't forget, in my lifetime, Mark Duggan nor Stephen Lawrence, or the terrible fire at Grenfell Tower, where 72 people died. This happened to mirror 9/11 in a really dark and conniving way, as we're now finding out more about what took place and the neglect and sharp practices that no governmental office wants to accept responsibility for. This disaster sparked a resounding wave of shock that moved Black people and other groups of people to support and organise across Britain.)

So, I moved to Balsall Heath, and once I finished school went to Cadbury VI Form College in Kings Norton. I then picked up two or three jobs. One in the new Bull Ring, working for £3.16 per hour... I won't even go into this as there's not enough space in this chapter! I was a waiter at the Hall Green Greyhound Racing Stadium and took up another casual role as what would be considered a steward in my college. Essentially, I was helping people find where they needed to go during open and induction days. This is how I met the mother of my first two children. I then decided to leave home to study Music Production and secured a house share with three other students in Sneinton, Nottingham for two years, which I intended to use to bypass the first year of university and join a music course at a university.

I moved back to Birmingham after briefly flirting with the idea of staying in the city longer, continuing to work in hospitality and later the bookies. I worked up to 50 hours a week whilst studying and trying to find time to socialise, all the while having a persistent feeling and undertone that time socialising was time that could be spent making money to cover rent and increase expenditure. I worked in clubs, pubs and for Interflora, where I became acquainted with a variety of flowers and arrangements whilst also utilising some of the listening skills I had learnt through my relationships during school, in situations where someone might be ordering flowers for a funeral. We accepted all sorts of orders, but those moments where someone is making an order and is crying openly as they pour their heart out into the choice of flower arrangement to send off their loved one are all about being kind and understanding. Makes me wonder who would be that person to do that for me after I'm gone…

By the way, when I say 'flirted', my girlfriend at the time and I were viewing houses as my study came to an end and the weeks until my rental agreement ran out. She signed on with an agency I was with and when she came up on the weekends we'd do some shifts together – this developed into spending four or five days together, sometimes a week at a time. We would generally alternate weekends travelling. She would come up from the Midlands and we would go down together, and I'd come back up either the Sunday night or earliest Monday morning as from memory, I feel I might have had a later lecture that day. Either that, or I'd miss it which I didn't want to make a habit of keeping.

I was very into my music and the pursuit of a career in it, having been producing my own backing tracks with electronic beats since meeting them in music classes in Year 7 via the old, colourful-backed Apple Macintosh and being introduced to them by Mr Knight, who passed not long after he left the school while I was in Year 10/11. I am not sure if it was known he was going to be leaving and what for, but I recall there being messages about his health. Rumours spread like wildfire in school, so you could never really tell what was what unless it was spoken about in assembly, and it had been a while. So much has happened since. The day we were informed was a shock, though being notified beforehand was a great way for the school to handle that container of emotion. I think it would have weighed far heavier if we'd been told out of the blue, which I think often affects the layers of grief we feel through our many different relationships and changes over time.

When I moved back to Birmingham, it was to Kings Heath, in a cosy one-bed flat above an estate agent on the High Street. I moved in with, by that time, my fiancée, and in that year I worked my arse off, trying to work as many hours as godly possible with a plan that I was going to university after my gap year, whilst still forsaking my time, energy and passion. We bought a studio set-up which sufficed for my producing practice. We bought a desk worth £800, a pair of monitors and an audio interface. Finance was a fairly easy option back then. Banks were giving away money in loans and debt in my late teens and early twenties. I do wonder about postcode associations and credit sometimes.

Looking back, I think I had an inherent independency nursed through my upbringing and psycho-dynamic between my father, stepfather, mother and I, where I could look after myself and others if I needed to. It was considered normal, all whilst deeply feeling that a connection was missing.

I actually met my father at 13 years of age. By then, I felt like it was already too late to feel anything, but I was open to getting to know him. We continue to talk to this day, mostly over the phone. And we meet occasionally, whether at my aunt's in London, at some family party, or on the off-chance we happen to meet when I'm in Birmingham, and go for days at a time rather than overnight visits when I go up to see my two elder children. I see my niece as she's not far from my mother's, and every time want to make time for a couple of friends, but there's just not enough time if they aren't available in the late evening – so we make do with phone calls for now. I either need to head back to London or have planned an afternoon train arriving so I can adjust before sleep. Self-care is real after those journeys, especially since the pandemic.

I also think part of this complex of missing connections manifests much of the time through withholding what I may have been feeling; the meaningful parts of me were hidden. "Oh, this person can see me. Stop, and turn back!!" I considered that intimacy was a feeling reserved for others as they were giving me their concerns as I took on a counsellor role in many of my friendships. A pattern that has replicated itself in my later life, and I only recently realised that I too have a need to express and be heard as well as feeling for and listening to another.

I volunteered for my local Samaritans training, and also became a Certified Counsellor so that I could open the door to understanding more about listening and communication dynamics as well as how to work with different types of relationships. I've been asking what type of relationship do I have with this person and whether is it appropriate for me to share? My inherent tendency leans towards allowing others to speak so that I can listen, and I find myself then feeding into opportunities to interject. Contributing to the overall exchange, rather than feeling the need to offload and scurry down the rabbit holes of the reasons behind our very existence.

For me, introspection assists with getting more clarity around my aims and desires. In these modern times where bias is often viewed as a thing we want to steer away from, I lean into considering how bias can work for me, and us, humanity on the whole. I think bias helps us to make better choices. Bias keeps us from straying from our path. Bias ensures that we focus on what matters most to us.

However, bias can also prevent us from having experiences that can broaden how we see the world and ourselves. As someone who spends time in meditation, contemplating the meaning of life, spending time evaluating my own choices and inherently, my own biases, I have been able to see how I too suffer from cognitive or unconscious bias. It's not a bad thing, it's just the brain's integrated way of shaping an environment that is as safe as possible.

Being the type of man I am, I often find myself at the periphery of conversations on race, being someone who has children with someone who is non-Black and in fact white. For me, understanding something about the nature of oppression through means that involve nationality has been a more subtle marker of the divide nonetheless present. Even that relationship was an example of multiple integrations; my partner's genes were a mix of English and Irish, nationalities that we were both aware had deep political tensions that had simmered somewhat by the time we met.

That relationship helped me to see further into the disparity of perspective on religious undertones. Being Catholic and Protestant, the huge historical rivalry between denominations in Britain, culminated in a relationship producing two children. Now we had the proof and produce of our interracial relationship. It's also on legal record. I was aware of ideas people had at the time around interracial relationships, and I didn't and still don't care for them. I recall before we got married, I brought my fiancée to a church that I occasionally went to as I enjoyed the vibe there.

In this particular church, we were pulled into the Pastor's office one day and advised not to live in the same house until we were married as "people in the church were saying things," and commenting on how bad it looked. We forced smiles and nodded in that meeting, and left confused and rejected. We never returned. They likely would not have expected us to come back. We already had a child and were expecting another, and yet we were meant to live apart for months while having a baby? If "God" doesn't want my relationship verified in the church through you, we would go somewhere else. And we did.

All of this, and I have to draw in and mention how much impact my skin colour has had on many relationships from school up to this day. Being dark-skinned was not always as cool as it is nowadays. I wouldn't say I was bullied, but my skin tone was the quick and easy go-to when making any retort directed at me.

This, from my school "friends".

This, from other Black children like me.

This, from people whom I felt saw me as different from them although we were shades of the same, being collectively 'Black'. I was just at the darker end of the colour chart of social race visibility which meant that my skin colour stood out.

I've had to remind myself that it wasn't my fault. People, let alone children, pick on seemingly easy targets. Hurt people can hurt people unwittingly, is what they say, and this is only too right when it comes to the transmutation of healing and self-realisation. But it would only go so far, as I wasn't a pushover for any physical interactions. You know the type, the hierarchy-establishing form of rough-play that pubescent teen boys with testosterone-overwhelm go through...

I spent more time defending others from being picked on or bullied. I knew that something wasn't right and did something about it. I made a difference, and although I may have got caught in the crossfire of race, ethnicity and colourism, I set an example of fairness and respect to some degree. I might be looking back at these situations with slightly rose-tinted glasses, but I do know that I defeat stereotypes every day.

I defeat stereotypes of fathers, young Black ones at that, who are separated from their children. I'm in my mid-thirties now, in a relationship with my youngest son's mother, claiming my self-love, mind and body fullness journey whilst still practising, seeing myself as a student of life and the people I meet. I have shared a snapshot of that journey on these pages.

I say all of this to show that I came from a background that could be described by many others as familiar, whether that's across the intersections of gender or race, or of family and economy. There are so many adults like myself who came from the same place who show up in various forms today.

I am typing this looking out of the window onto the main road, currently manifesting a new place. We recently began redecorating as it approaches Christmas of 2022. Our first Christmas on the other side of the pandemic, and hopefully our last Christmas in this place. We have plans to expand, and to expand, we need space to do so freely and securely within an environment that embraces that.

So, here's to considered choices being made – not necessarily more – but choices more in line with wholesome intent and passion fulfilment. If there is anything I would like for anybody to take from this chapter, it's that they can live their life authentically without being an "influencer", celebrity, or whatever that depiction of the rich and famous is. We can humanise ourselves and each other without judgement, and give credit to ourselves and others on a multitude of levels. Why not explore those connections and grow with them into relationships where we can pour into each other's cup, instead of stealing time and energy from them with resistance? Knowing that I would rather know something than not, whilst exploring and respecting boundaries, helps me maintain a balance. If I ever need to upset the balance, it's done by informing with mutual agreement, intention, and clear direction.

Kintsugi

by Dr Bijna Kotak Dasani MBE FRSA

Kintsugi: *Japan's ancient art of embracing imperfections lends itself to a broader philosophy of embracing the beauty of human flaws. The 15th-century practice of kintsugi, meaning "to join with gold", is a reminder to stay optimistic when things fall apart and to celebrate the flaws and missteps of life.*

I am the eldest born of Indian-origin parents who were themselves born in East Africa and moved to the United Kingdom soon before the Ugandan Exodus. Whilst I was born and raised in Leicester, in the heart of England, I have a significant influence of African, English, and Indian heritage and culture in my life to varying measures.

Intersectionality shows us that social identities work on multiple levels, resulting in unique experiences, opportunities, but also barriers for each person. For me, this combination of heritage, social norms and cultural expectation has resulted in exactly that.

Being a British female of Indian origin and African descent has been an enriching experience. I have found the journey extremely valuable and fulfilling, yet paradoxically, there have been moments of extreme adversity. The cultural and social expectations (around gender-based norms) of women from ethnic minority backgrounds are intertwined and can prove to be challenging at times.

As such, one of the main factors was living up to a persona of 'expectation' (societal), vs. a persona of 'authenticity' (personal), which would have enabled me to live in a way that allowed kindness and compassion towards myself, first and foremost.

This catalysed my interest in the spectrum of Diversity, Equity, and Inclusion (DE&I) both within my professional and personal life, so I could understand the implications of my intersectionality and why the status quo was necessary/ existential.

These experiences led me to the path of self-discovery across the spectrum. Today, I share my learnings through the work I am committed to, in raising awareness and education on the spectrum of topics within DE&I – with organisations and individuals globally.

I was recently humbled with the title of one of 'the most Dynamic Business Personalities (2022)' by Fortune India and reflected on this deeply. In the eyes of the world, I stand as someone who has been appreciated by universities, with an Honorary Doctorate; by Royalty – Her Majesty Queen Elizabeth II, and HH Sheikh Saif bin Zayed Al Nahyan, UAE; and global investment banks, such as Morgan Stanley who honoured me for a week on Times Square as their Diversity Advocate of the Year.

At the tip of the iceberg, what's visible is that I am an Ivy-league educated, award-winning ethnic minority woman who has broken through many glass ceilings, addressed audiences across the world, attained significant cultural exposure by living and working globally; London Wall to Wall Street and beyond. And I have also had the humbling privilege of serving monarchies.

Today, having spent over two decades in the global financial services industry, which is an industry that remains largely male-dominated (and lacks overall diversity), at C-suite level, I have transitioned to a portfolio career. I am advising boards and CEOs in the Venture Capital ecosystem, and exploring opportunities to create opportunities for sustainable inclusive capital practices.

Underneath the iceberg, is a different narrative, one which I am constantly and consciously working to strengthen through a deeper understanding of past traumas, and also the refinement of present practices as pillars for a strengthened future.

My journey is that of an introverted female of heritage where traditional value systems imply women and men are measured against different baselines. Raised within a traditional culture-influenced value system, tolerance and compromise were parts of my DNA. However, I learned through challenging scenarios of my journey, that anything in excess, void of firm boundaries, signals that unreasonable treatment (towards another) is acceptable.

The more research I did, the more I learnt about the significant correlation between ethnic minority women and (generational and gender-based) trauma.

As a survivor of multiple post-traumatic brain injuries and having recovered from emotional, economic, psychological, and physical trauma and complex post-traumatic stress disorder (PTSD), I started to explore the complexities of the overlap between Intersectionality in the context of DE&I.

Trauma has many physiological side effects and can impact everything from memory and concentration, to dysregulation of the nervous system, digestive ailments, panic attacks and nightmares, feelings of unpredictability, distrust, self-repent and even self-harm.

The World Health Organisation (WHO) estimates that globally, almost one million people a year take their own life.[1] For every suicide, there are many others attempting suicide and even more have serious thoughts of suicide. Millions of people suffer intense grief or are otherwise profoundly impacted by suicidal behaviours.

There is a fine line between having the strength to face the adversity of social and cultural expectations, and associated taboos, labels, and judgements – and tipping over to a point of no return where you lean on every ounce of energy within your body and soul – in an attempt to savour or end your own life.

[1] https://www.who.int/news-room/fact-sheets/detail/suicide

This usually happens when we feel we are alive on the surface which is visible, yet experience gradual death by trauma, emotional or otherwise, but not as visible.

In this life, underneath the iceberg, the circumstances I faced led me to challenging and changing my entire world as I knew it.

This became the pinnacle of translating pain into power, and, over time, I developed a relationship with my internal self to harness and nurture my internal well-being and redefine my existence, entirely void of social and cultural vulnerabilities.

I adore and enjoy multiple aspects of my heritage, faith and culture, and these will always be key parts of my unique identity and drivers of my impact during my lifetime. If embraced correctly, I have learned they can make life limitless!

Overall, it has been a conscious, strategic, and intense exercise to reconcile my internal narrative to that of the one that is visible externally, at the tip of the iceberg. Mindfulness is priceless.

I am grateful every single day for all that this world and life has to offer. During my most turbulent times, I have been blessed with the kindest of souls and gestures who, knowingly and unknowingly, have given me strength through their words, wisdom and guidance.

From colleagues to friends, family and everyone in between, I have become increasingly conscious of the energies I choose to keep close. These are the people whom I respect for their honest and, advocacy – especially in my absence, integrity and unconditional support – even when I explicitly ask for it.

This is where my professional and personal identities have sometimes intertwined; some of the most incredible leaders I have had the privilege of working with and learning from still remain mentors and guides, and some have been saviours. Friends and family who have been authentic and kind now operate as colleagues / professional partners too.

Seeing my mother's transition in the UK from Africa, the adjustments she made for social and cultural norms during my childhood – whilst maintaining her own career in financial services and raising a family – and her unconditional support through my journey, had a significant impact on my independent and ambitious choices. She has inspired me immensely.

However, through my outreach work in the community, I have learned many ethic minority women are unable to deviate from traditional gender-based norms and expectations even today.

Research[2] shows that embedding fear is the most widely used form of manipulation; partnered with imagination, it is the mother of control.

Fear is the biggest ally of manipulation that continues to drive gender-based violence and is dominant across ethnic minority groups all over the world. It is consciously and subconsciously played into mechanisms of stigma, taboo, and societal conformity.

[2] https://sofoarchon.com/fear-based-manipulation/

But in the end, some people hide their sins, and some hide their shadows.

Wouldn't it be beautiful if we lived in a world where human beings were embraced for their differences and celebrated for being able to fulfil their lives and journeys through their identities?!

In the famous words of Maya Angelou, *'And still, I rise...'*

Whilst I have absolute appreciation of professional and personal milestones, my view today is more about achieving a philosophy that underpins all milestones.

Life occurs in stages; survival, transformation, growth. Within each one, we are different versions of ourselves. At each stage, I have much to reflect upon and be thankful for, but ultimately, I would never succeed in any of these stages without the positive influences and individuals in my life at each point in time.

> *'I thank those who have bestowed positivity*
> *and love towards me ... and those who haven't*
> *For the moments that gave way to laughter ...*
> *and those which led to tears*
> *For the times that made memories ...*
> *and those which left anxieties*
> *For each and every aspect taught me something valuable,*
> *gave me clarity, and helped me to cleanse my life*
> *both physically and emotionally.'*
>
> *Bijna*

To be able to move forward, it is important to close circles and chapters when necessary and leave the past in the past, whilst carrying the lessons and learning in your toolkit for the future.

And all this means a world I am content with; a very simple form of being where I am consciously practicing measures for my own evolution, maintaining my own vibrational frequency and clear on boundaries where energies and circumstances are not in synch for me.

It takes immense courage to spend even a moment in an environment that is detrimental to one's mental health … and it takes all the courage in the world to either walk towards physical suicide or the cultural and social suicide of exiting a toxic environment and making one's entire existence crumble in the process.

Instead of accentuating social pressures, integrity towards those who need compassion is the difference that can light a candle of hope in the heart of someone who is emotionally lost to the pain of otherwise invisible wounds.

Understanding this and creating areas of psychological safety can literally help save lives. Any disruptor who can advocate for a new approach to stigma and taboo as well as educating others on the importance of embracing support for mental health – particularly for ethnic minorities and women – will be greatly valued.

My DE&I research has been reinforced (through data and studies) that many cultures still normalise judgements, labelling, direct and indirect coercion, and abuse. It becomes a part of daily behaviour which is reinforced by similar practices in their societies which then operate as echo chambers.

For example, there is significant coercion through triangulation between various members of an extended family in joint family practices, often the daughter or daughter-in-law, creating agreement and alignment against all odds, for example – particularly in ethnic minority settings.

When I was experiencing my trauma, my GP was my most powerful disruptor, as was as my employer. Another patient at the same medical practice sadly lost her life the same day I lost my eyesight (temporarily) and was fighting for my life. Subsequently an investigation was launched by the state against my perpetrator.

We were both of a similar age, in similar circumstances, similarly concerned about the social implications to our families if we failed to make 'things work'. The difference was that I had disruptors who held me through the period that was to follow with reinforced commitment and care.

The greatest push was that my journey needed to be addressed appropriately by the justice system – it's a very fine line between surviving and becoming a name in the list of half a million women who are killed by their family members / partners worldwide globally every year.

Anyone that can apply empathy and integrity towards those who need us and choose compassion versus accentuating social pressures can **literally** help save lives.

When we start to share our experiences, we release ourselves from the versions we created to survive and evolve towards versions that will also help others to thrive! It's far from easy, but ultimately there is an art to graciousness, and through it emitting strength and vulnerability in equal measure.

My legacy today is that of embracing my reality and learning to help raise awareness and education for a shift in approach across the verticals of DE&I – we can all make subtle differences at home and at work through being kind. It takes mass evolution for a revolution, but I want to help change the narrative one step at a time.

Differences should be the seed of positivity and power, not (perceived) weakness. My work on DE&I is an enabler for positivity across cultures, industries and sectors. Our existence deserves to be limitless.

Women and girls are still not permitted to study or work in many parts of the world. This paralyses them economically and later in life makes them susceptible to economic abuse – which is an extension of other forms of abuse, control, and coercion. As recently as the late 1980s, it was normal (in certain industries and economies) to expect women to resign from roles if they chose to marry (but not the same for men), and today over 130 million girls are not 'permitted' to attend school.

There is a major gap in STEM – female representation is less than 30% globally but over 75% of roles in the next five years will require STEM skills. So without the right training and education, the gap will continue to widen; however, firms, societies and nations can address this by reskilling and upskilling women of working age, and encourage education for the next and upcoming generation. Digital literacy is also a key component, especially as FinTech capabilities can help create financial equality. In fact , we are already seeing incredible advances in rural communities being catalysed in fast-growing economies like Africa and India.

In fact, this year's International Women's Day (IWD) 2023 theme, as set out by the United Nations, was to explore the impact of the digital gender gap on widening economic and social inequalities – and spotlight the importance of protecting the rights of women and girls in digital spaces, and addressing online and ICT-facilitated gender-based violence.

I would encourage women and girls to prioritise their own learning and development as education is empowering and goes hand in glove with economic capability, literacy and equality.

Whilst the quest for equality and opportunity will (for our foreseeable future) have clarity to various degrees of granularity, the time to act is NOW.

Sometimes it's a challenge to do this in difficult circumstances but ultimately, we can find allies – I have benefitted hugely from the support of male and female allies at work and in my close circle for friends.

Women are the queens who help others fix their crowns; let's come together and rise in the spirit of contribution, as opposed to competition.

To quote the great Maya Angelou one more time, *"Each time a woman stands up for herself, without knowing it possibly, without claiming it, she stands up for all women."*

We must preserve our power, choose ourselves and above all …

… let our love for ourselves, our purpose, and our evolution and existence be greater than our fear!

Let's Be Honest and Change Perceptions and Expectations

by Kate Wilson

L et me first introduce myself. My name is Kate Wilson. I am a career-focused, mother of three beautiful girls, who has a dream. That dream is to inspire the next generation of females to be confident, ambitious, resilient individuals who strive to achieve in the workplace. Whatever career path they choose, and whatever their workplace looks like in the future, I want them to have the courage to think outside the box, lead, break into industries that are traditionally associated with males, and become financially independent.

However, what I won't say to them is, that the path to career success will be easy and without its challenges. I will not tell them that life will be plain sailing, and that their capability won't be judged simply because of gender at times. I will not tell them that they will not face relationship and power struggles along the way, and I will also not say that it won't be an exhausting juggling act at times. But what I will tell them is, that battling through the unpredictable and arduous career journey to accomplish their version of success will be 100% worth it, and something to be bloody well proud of!

We often hear that famous saying 'You can have it all' – a popular phrase that is banded about frequently referring to the somewhat expected 'traditional' phases of life deemed necessary for women to experience, particularly in Westernised societies. We somehow grow up and sleepwalk into thinking that once we finish school, we should go on to higher education, get a job, find a lifelong partner, get married, raise a family – and all of this whilst continuing on the progressive career trajectory demanded of the 21st century. By the way, we then normalise that this immense undertaking is possible whilst also striking the perfect, happy and healthy work-life balance, with complete mental stability.

Well, I am sorry to have to be the one to tell you this, but this whole concept is a myth, a legend that has been created over time, much like the Loch Ness Monster and Robin Hood. It is my view that we are promoting habits and behaviours that were endured and associated with a very different, slower-paced, less materialistic, past world. The lived experience of women in the past is not necessarily suited to the career women of today, nor can it be expected to be. It is called evolution. Despite what 'tag lines' we are told about equality, and the very positive advancements that have taken place, we are still not where we should be, and there is still a lot of work to do.

Before hitting my late twenties when I had my first child, I did not think anything of the 'You can have it all' phrase. In fact, I remember thinking it would be easy, with a bit of hard work. At this time in my life, I was part of the Operational Support Unit in Merseyside Police, and was one of two younger women working in a very male-dominated environment. I recall a time sitting in the riot van waiting to be deployed on a search, working long hours due to a serious incident in the area. We were having a laugh, joking around like we always did to detract from the seriousness of the job we were doing, when suddenly one of the lads got a call from his wife. The whole van could not help but hear the call of desperation even if we did not want to. The lady on the phone was crying and frustrated because she had been at home all day, with two very young children and was due to go to work. She wanted some support, and was begging him to come home and take over the parenting responsibilities.

It was not possible for him, given the nature of the job we were on. Much to my naivety at the time, I regretfully said, 'What is she complaining about? You have been at work all day earning extra money, and she is just sat at home with the kids.' Something that I now know from experience was completely inappropriate to think. He was by no means the only one from our section that got this type of SOS call on a regular basis. A lot of the lads had kids and working partners, and I underestimated the pressure that came with this family dynamic.

Now in my late thirties, with an established career in cybersecurity, having three young children, and attempting to hold down relationships, whilst being everything to everyone, and wanting to progress, now means I resonate with the 'You can have it all' phrase, but not in a good way. The fact that this ideal is still imparted creates a sense of anger and frustration inside my body. For me, this term is deceptive and a falsified narrative put out there in the media for attention. If you asked me what mental image this triggers, for me it would be social media posts of a woman showboating that she is a successful business lady, powerful, looks amazing, has numerous children, cooks dinner from home-grown, fresh produce that she picks herself every morning, then food preps for the family for the next week or two. She claims to be up at 5 a.m. every day, trains hard in the gym, does her own cleaning, has an impeccable house and even alleges to be a devoted wife, who home educates her children, whilst even having a pet, or ten, thrown into the mix as well.

And breathe. Gosh, it was exhausting writing that never-ending list of perceived perfection, let alone living it! Of course, I have over-exaggerated here, but it helps to get my point across. Let's face it, living this full-on life would be somewhat strenuous, energy-draining and completely unattainable, not the happy, balanced, fulfilling lifestyle that is being portrayed. The good news is there are more and more women recognising and vocalising the fact that you can't have it all. In my view, those who pretend they can, are doing women an injustice. This is not women supporting women, but instead a competitive nonsense that invokes immense pressure on females and is detrimental to mental well-being and physical health. Not only that, but this distorted perception is counter-intuitive when it comes to trying to achieve gender parity in the workplace. So, how can we break the bias, influence change and support career women?

In my view, an honest approach is needed. We should consistently share positive and negative experiences, be frank about the challenges that come with being an ambitious woman, and understand the contradictory societal pressures that exist today. If 'preparation is the key to success', then forewarning young women about the potential hurdles they will face, and providing them with education to help them navigate the challenges to then cope and thrive, will empower women to be impactive, to go out there and grab opportunities, and confront the challenges head-on.

To understand where my head is at when I say 'contradictory societal pressures', let me share some thoughts and observations with you.

'You should not define yourself by your career'

Yet, from nursery school age, we ask our children, 'What do you want to be when you grow up?', and moreover teenagers are asked to make life-impacting decisions about which subjects to study to align with the requirements of their desired career choice. The whole education system is geared up and focused on identifying a desired occupation. So who is anyone to say, we should not define ourselves by our careers, given most of our life is spent preparing for the workplace, and we know that people often spend more time with colleagues than with their own family.

'It is okay to be a stay-at-home mum'

Yet, if a teenage girl went to a careers advisor and said she wanted to be a stay-at-home mum when she grows up, I very much doubt it would be taken seriously, or even accepted. I do not envisage (or though I could be wrong) there is a careers section dedicated to advising on this as an option. In fact, let's go one step further... what if that same teenager was, in fact, male, and he said that he wanted to be a stay-at-home dad to support his career-driven partner? Again, I am sure this would raise a few eyebrows, and he would be encouraged to think again.

'You will not be judged by what you look like, and appearances shouldn't matter'

Yet, psychology tells us that regardless of gender, we have seven seconds to make a good first impression, and this is often related to our appearance and body language. As women, we have to consider if we are wearing too much make-up, or not wearing enough. Have we picked clothes that are too revealing, too tight, or alternatively do not look smart or professional enough? Will we be taken seriously or judged if we do not meet the expectations of others?

'Being intelligent is cool and attractive'

Yet, in schools, we do not promote the fact that intelligence is multifaceted and that there are numerous types, but instead are bound by the outdated, rigid education system which can leave extremely intelligent individuals believing they are not clever simply because maths and English are not their strongest subjects. According to psychologist Howard

Gardner, there are numerous types of intelligence including linguistic-verbal intelligence and body-kinaesthetic intelligence, to name but a few. Also, reality TV has glamorised appearing not to be clever, silently promoting that by coming across as uneducated and relying on looks alone will make you popular and quickly earn you a fortune overnight – something which should be recognised as being highly misleading, and insincere.

Now you have read these observations, pause and think about the mixed messages being given. Of course, there are many more, and I challenge you to think of some others from your own experiences.

For me, these are good examples, that show these confused narratives are not only unhelpful, but are fuelling people's unconscious and conscious biases e.g. if a young woman is overtly clever, then she may not be seen as cool or attractive, and so she may play down her intellect as a result of peer pressure. Or, an ambitious, career-driven woman may not be seen as a dedicated mother, because she is so focused on her work. This one I have experienced personally. I once said to a colleague, 'I want to go for promotion'. The said colleague happened to be a white middle-aged male, whose wife stayed at home to support the family of four, whilst he openly climbed the career ladder. He had a very traditional home set-up. When I shared my desire for promotion I was met with, 'No, you don't, you've got a young family,' implying I had to choose between one and the other. I was lost for words, stunned at what I had heard. There was no malicious intent, but it was clear as day there was an element of unconscious bias and judgement being made. If I were male, I am confident that he would have not even thought of saying this.

Now, let's move on to the confidence gap. I think that when organisations think about how they can promote gender equality and encourage women to climb the ladder, there is a misconception that the gap that exists is owning to maternity issues and childcare only. The actual psychological and biological differences are often overlooked, with the confidence gap being one.

So what is it? The term was coined by Dr Russ Harris, and attempts to explain some of the underlying psychological reasons why men tend to outperform women in the workplace, despite women actually performing better academically. The key factor – yes, you guessed it – is confidence, or lack of it. Research on this topic also suggests a correlation between the confidence gap and a reduced tendency to negotiate, receive a pay rise and achieve leadership roles. I also think that there is prejudice and biases that exist, that cause women difficulty at times. For example, a woman who is assertive can be mislabelled as being aggressive, particularly if they are speaking up on a topic that may challenge a team or peer. A woman in a leadership role can be labelled as 'a bitch' if they are stricter in their approach, straight-talking and question a decision, yet the same interpretation does not often happen if a male leader shows the same traits. It is usually associated with him being a strong and decisive leader. So if a more junior female member of staff is hearing this type of language, then it could easily hinder self-confidence and dampen career aspirations.

How strong, decisive and fearless women are perceived as aggressive or a threat could quite easily be a contributing factor to the worrying statistics around women in leadership.

Women Count is a major annual report that looks at the number of women on Executive Committees in the FTSE 350. It has tracked the gender diversity of British business for the past seven years. Concerningly, data reveals that 96% of Chief Executive Officers (CEOs) in the FTSE 350 are men, evidencing the disparity that occurs between men and women at the top of British business, despite entry-level recruitment often being close to 50:50. It is clear that gender parity is facing an uphill struggle, and organisations are overlooking and/or failing to attract and retain the diverse talent that is out there.

So why is this? I think this is because there is a lack of consideration and understanding about the different challenges that women face in the workplace, from hormonal changes such as periods and the menopause, to female health issues, for example, endometriosis and polycystic ovaries. Then there are psychological differences such as imposter syndrome and confidence, in addition to logistical matters, such as childcare and care-giving responsibilities. Then there are conscious and unconscious biases. I have already shared with you that people have told me that I don't want/shouldn't think of promotion because I have children and should focus on them, instead of striving to financially provide for my family. I also question why someone I barely know feels it is okay to tell me what I do or do not want, based on my personal circumstances.

I have been called aggressive and intimidating because I have challenged decisions and behaviours in a constructive and assertive manner. In my policing days, I was often told that I had only been successful at times because I was the 'token bird', or 'easy on the eye', rather than being credited for my ideas, determination and courage. Finally, I have been mistaken for an admin assistant on more than once occasion, rather than the expert speaker at events. All of this could just be because I have a northern accent, like humour, wear make-up, love the salon and have a bit of fake tan. So how could it be that I am also a Subject Matter Expert in Serious and Organised Crime, have a master's degree and am an action film, car-loving, sports enthusiast?

I jest, of course, but the reality is that people do have preconceived ideas about females in the workplace, and what career choices they should make, and are very opinionated about how they should live their lives, making judgements if it goes against traditional standards. This can be limiting and cause obstruction to career advancement, and confidence levels, and dampen creative thinking. We may be part of the same human race, but our lived experiences are very different. Helping women to succeed and thrive in the workplace is not just about equal pay and maternity rights. It is about understanding the multifaceted challenges they face, and the societal pressures and biases that they encounter, adapting and supporting each other, regardless of gender, or any other protected feature.

In an effort to support women, I have started a positive movement on social media called SHEisBOSSingit, whereby the content is designed to educate, motivate and inspire. The work I am undertaking to influence change is on top of my day job, but is needed, and a real passion of mine, given my own experiences, and hearing about the challenges other women have faced. It is not easy, but do not let ignorance and prejudice prevent you from reaching your goals and dreaming big; we need positive role models and allies in this space, and I encourage you to be one.

Just

by Emma Jones

"Emma, you *just* make everyone else you work with look terrible at their job."

That was quite the compliment to receive from my line manager! It was said during a speech at a customary 'leaving drinks' event, to mark my upcoming transition into a new role. Whilst laughing and reminiscing, my manager went on to say my departure meant everyone could go back to their 'averagely performing selves'. Although it was a light-hearted (albeit slightly awkward) few seconds on my part, these comments marked a pivotal moment in my life.

There have been countless instances where comments were made to me with some sort of negative context or undertone. Whilst sometimes intentional, and sometimes not, discriminatory and shrewd statements have featured heavily throughout my personal and professional life for as long as I can remember. Thereby allowing my fears of being disliked and judged simply for being me, alongside this looming negativity, to remain.

So why, of all the moments (my 'moving moment' as I like to call it), did this one mean so much? Well, it marked a stark realisation that every difficult encounter in my career was never actually about me. The subtle discrimination, unnecessary challenges, and incomprehensible setbacks were all a reflection of those whose behaviour it originated from. It said much more about those individuals and the institutions they represented rather than me. For the first time, it was clear that nothing was, and never will be, personal. This is the most valuable life lesson I could have ever learned. One which is responsible for entirely reframing my approach to breaking bias.

Lesson #1: Nothing is ever personal.

"Just"

This simple word has been a huge part of my day-to-day, and not only because of my desire for everything in life to be just! What has become obvious lately is that this is a word also used to try to soften a message. It is almost a way to excuse what is being said, indirectly apologise in advance, or subconsciously gain permission for the content that follows. Until now, I never considered the way the term can alter the delivery of a message.

On the surface, it can make you feel as though the person saying it to you has your best interests at heart and means no harm. Now, I am not so convinced.

Lesson #2: Say goodbye to that four-letter adverb; no more "just".

"I have been bullying Emma *just* because."

Self-awareness is recognised in many ways as a factor associated with our ability to connect with others. So much that happens in our past lives, accounts for who we are today. Being bullied in primary school for no legitimate reason meant I knew what it felt like from a young age to suffer due to not conforming to another person's expectations. It taught me so much about difference and triggered my focus on fairness. That feeling of confusion and isolation has never faded; the thought of anyone feeling that way is too much. Maybe this explains my innate desire to take on other people's injustices, which is hard to step back from at times.

As a teen in the early noughties, growing up in north-west England, young people were commonly referred to as 'yobs'. There were endless sweeping generalised statements about the 'youth of today' and the Anti-Social Behaviour Order (ASBO) era was firmly in full swing. I was offended! Offended because by being a young person, there was an automatic assumption by many that the youth were up to no good or were creating problems for society. There was little positivity about my generation, and I felt that needed to be challenged. Having embraced charity work during secondary school, I became the recipient of a local award

– Young Citizen of the Year – and worked for subsequent years with high school students to discuss how to volunteer and the benefits of doing so.

My mid-teenage years also included a role chairing a youth advisory group for the local police authority. From the design of knife amnesties to representing the views of others throughout the community, this position included working alongside other advisory groups. As a collective, we were consulted on current projects, such as the implementation of body scanners, and were invited to provide our perspectives to ensure policing proposals were considerate of the community they were intended to serve.

This was the first time I was directly exposed to the issues faced by ethnic groups and LGBTQ+ persons. This exposure was shocking at times, but incredibly insightful and taught me the significance of always remaining open-minded. Later in my career, sharing these stories has been a way of bringing context to related conversations, to help others realise the importance of knowing what you do not know.

Lesson #3: Get comfortable with being uncomfortable, pronto.

"That is *just* one person's experience, Emma."

From my early twenties and up until my 'moving moment', I spent years focused on trying to bring people together and advocating for inclusion. It was alongside my day job and predominantly in my spare time. For the most part, I put aside my own lived experiences of bias and toxic cultures in favour of an approach focused on advocacy. To an extent, you could say those experiences were buried in the 'big picture' and I had to hope that behaving in such a way would affect positive future change.

There were two significant reasons for taking this position and keeping such personal experiences to myself.

Firstly, I was conscious that many viewed me as an individual who was still achieving and progressing well in the workplace. Whilst some colleagues unhelpfully attributed this to my gender, physical appearance, and lack of children, I was very driven and wanted to be a successful individual.

Secondly, there was a genuine uncertainty as to whether anyone would listen or understand the real impact of such behaviours. Ultimately, many environments and even communities still now have the unwritten rule of 'shut up and put up' which fuelled my belief that the only way to accomplish change was to be thematic, to present required action in a way which was wholly forward-thinking, rather than being seen to reside on individual examples. I did not want to be perceived as the common denominator or exemplify a stereotype of someone pushing an agenda for personal reasons instead of for the cause. I was already acutely aware of the need to "prove [myself] twice over as a young woman" and knew within my organisation weakness was not tolerated.

Lesson #4: We all have self-limiting beliefs; we must acknowledge them to overcome them.

"I *just* do not understand why you put so much effort into the inclusion work, Emma. Everyone knows you are competent, so what is the point?"

Whilst there was never any judgement of those who wished to stay silent on the topic of inclusion or their own personal experiences with bias, what saddened me was witnessing the way such an important conversation was interpreted by others. Some not only refused to acknowledge the importance of speaking openly on bias as a topic, but also did not appreciate the courage it took to stand up and speak. This fuelled my own standpoint.

As someone trying to tackle bias alongside my primary role with very little time to generate change, advocacy was the only method that felt productive. I was compounded on a few occasions where I drew on personal experiences, only to receive criticism, gaslighting, and dismissive reactions. Refraining from sharing personal instances is certainly not my approach of choice now, and reflecting on this time is tough. However, it taught me the value of balance. Articulating vision with positivity as well as individual experience adds depth and realism to the diversity and inclusion conversation in the same way it does with any topic. It is your 'why'.

Lesson #5: Lived experience is evidence of a person's reality.

"That is *just* the way it has always been done, Emma."

A purely thematic approach was not wrong despite my personal reflections. Ultimately, the intention of advocating for inclusivity was to create and maintain inclusive cultures to enable everyone to safely be themselves without adverse impact. I have never been an expert in this arena, but I always had a deep desire to improve the lives of others in whichever way possible rather than dedicate my efforts to a certain characteristic. For me, it was, and still is, about putting people first. Understanding their perspective, listening intently, and unremitting attention to detail. My work has spanned local and national initiatives both for one-time instances and continuous long-term projects.

As a people manager, in professional and voluntary settings, it is my mission to really get to know others. Within various teams, I lead previously unheard-of conversations about neurodiversity, flexible working, workplace adjustments, and mental health. This is a pivotal part of creating safe spaces for individuals to speak openly on a one-to-one basis with the assurance they will be heard and seen.

I have spent time in many different roles, always instilling these approaches directly or via the coaching of my peers. As a manager and leader, it is my ambition to raise awareness and generate conversation to embrace perspectives and to help others learn rather than tell them what needs to be done.

There were periods in my career when colleagues mocked my style and the amount of time spent on staff matters, and I found myself excluded from certain forums due to these more 'modern' methods. In addition, feedback loops rarely existed, so there was no way to validate whether the people that mattered most, my staff, were feeling the benefit. However, as my tenure passed, my self-belief grew, and I became less concerned by the unhelpful views of others and dedicated my actions to simply trying to do the right thing in any given setting. It seems this mantra has worked okay so far.

Lesson #6: Any activity that contributes to improving the lives of others is worthwhile, no matter how big or small.

"Emma, the diversity work is *just* a 'nice' to do."

A few years ago, an opportunity arose to lead a national, organisation-wide diversity group dedicated to the protected characteristic of age. As age is all-encompassing, and uniquely affects us all, it has oftentimes been overlooked.

It may come as no surprise that I felt it was an opportunity to raise awareness and prompt change which could not be missed. People would probably expect me to focus solely on young people given my 'millennial' identification, but that was never the intention. Age divides are deepened when we only target certain generations. Of course, tailored activities reflecting generational challenges are vital, but for me, the real strengthening of an age-inclusive culture lies in breaking down barriers, increasing understanding, and operating with togetherness. The launching of events showcasing the need for age-inclusive language, the creation of new working practices, and the celebration of the annual intergenerational awareness week, was exciting. Seeing a group and cause gain momentum not previously experienced really proved the power of dedicated networks in reaching others.

There was no way it could just stop there. With a spotlight on intersectionality, now was an ideal time to partner with other diversity group leads to propose and support formal schemes, such as mentoring and talent programmes. 'Knowledge is power' is a phrase encountered frequently in many industries, but in all honesty, I often found it difficult to resonate with. Knowledge shared is the real force for good, the real power, so that was what all diversity group leaders aimed to embody. Together we knew what needed to be done, we had collective insights, and we recognised the pioneering position we were in to have our recommendations put into practice to benefit everyone. A 'need' to do, not a 'nice' to do.

Lesson 7: Never underestimate the privilege associated with having a platform to represent those who cannot represent themselves.

Finally Saying Goodbye to "*Just*"!

That life lesson, about nothing ever being personal, has a lot to answer for. Not only did it change my approach to breaking bias and progressing inclusion initiatives, but it also spurred me into a different kind of action. I took the plunge and started to share my lived experiences, constructively, with those organisations that needed to hear them. It even came as a surprise to some in all sectors that bias, discrimination, and microaggressions are still very much a part of many people's present. Fortunately, this realisation appears to have revived a conversation, instigated reviews, and driven several continuous efforts to improve corresponding cultures.

At the very least, my openness helped provide a baseline understanding and contributed to the tracking of tangible progress. Ironically, individuals wishing to engage with me on the topics of bias, diversity, and inclusion, have increased substantially. For me, this was when the value of disclosing a personal story was realised. I only wish I had done it sooner.

Lesson #8: The opportunity to unapologetically speak your truth does not come around often, so seize it.

My Cyber Calling

My path changed dramatically upon being posted to a national law enforcement cyber team following a successful promotion process. This proved to be at the hands of a forward-thinking leader who recognised my transferable, rather than technical, skills at the time.

This opportunity enabled my move into an industry where I **finally** feel I belong. The cybersecurity sector benefits profusely from the very fact it is a relatively new, innovative discipline, that largely recognises the need for people from all walks of life to counter the threat and protect the masses from those who seek to disrupt, undermine, and harm our societies. Unsurprisingly though, the field struggles to even achieve diverse representation and therefore proactive inclusivity efforts take a back seat, often under the guise of existing cultures feeling 'organically inclusive'.

The cyber industry is always open to innovation and new ways of working, so it was the perfect opportunity to raise the profile of everyday inclusion – what to do and how to do it. I began efforts to develop regional inclusion networks, host topical drop-in sessions, and implement numerous changes to working practices in a bid to be more considerate of others. In doing so, I discovered some of the best practices recommended had never been heard of. I even found myself speaking in forums where attendees were being exposed to this type of information for the very first time; the use of pronouns, neurodiversity in the workplace, well-being, and inclusive language being just a few.

It dawned on me quite early that the cybersecurity and inclusion topics were very similar in how they were perceived. Basically, they resonated the most with those who have an explicit understanding, and very little with those who think these efforts are the responsibility of someone else. This understanding spurred me to act, and I relished the chance to bring inclusion to cyber by giving a presentation at an infamous global cybersecurity conference. In the first of its kind, this session aimed to initiate intentional inclusion by explicitly detailing how inclusive practices directly influence the effectiveness of a team in responding to a cyber incident. Excitingly, the presentation has since led to a series of corresponding events planned for upcoming years centred on this theme. Taking a chance on a novel topic was daunting. Although, once I accepted that people attended or watched online because they wanted to hear what I had to say, rather than pick it apart, the game changed.

Lesson #9: Make sure people know that inclusion is not about having to get it right all the time; being open and willing to learn is far more progressive.

Being Who I Once Needed Most

Acting on the hindsight that sharing personal experiences is not weak has led me to dedicate much of my time recently to specific female and STEM (science, technology, engineering, maths) activities. It is important now more than ever to channel my efforts into both achieving diverse representation in the sector and retaining talent with inclusive workplaces.

Speaking to women in cyber events has enabled me to discuss candidly my viewpoints, as well as highlight the vast support available to women in the sector. I still find myself being the only woman in the room far too often than is acceptable, so we all have a part to play in addressing that imbalance. This includes being more open and transparent about available career opportunities and recruiting based on core skill sets rather than previously demonstrated competencies. It is vital we bust all the myths held about the industry, starting with those centred around the absolute need for prescribed technical qualifications. I am yet to obtain one of those and seem to be doing just fine. As do the cybercriminals!

Being visible to others is not solely about the here and now. Presenting at schools in socially disadvantaged locations has helped to expose young adults to how accessible technology careers are, as well as learn what they can do to succeed in the workplace. It still astonishes me how my accent still generates questions regarding the reality of success outside of London! Volunteering with several charities to nurture the next generation of talent continues to be essential. It is a pleasure to facilitate conversations and deliver activities to pique their interest and passion from the age of 4 to 18. Above everything else, addressing the topic of difference is a key component to enabling the workforce today and, in the decades to come. Instilling the very fact that with difference comes Dynamics, Depth, and Discovery, has become my overarching message.

Lesson #10: People believe they cannot be what they cannot see.

If there is one thing I aspire to achieve for the future, it is to highlight the 'how' element when it comes to achieving inclusivity. It is too often overlooked. Whilst people can be told what needs to be done specifically, there is never really a conversation about the steps required every single day, in every interaction, and when facing every task regardless of the context. That aspect of the discussion currently seems to sit firmly in the 'too difficult' box. Now is the time to adopt a simple, but significant mindset and be intentional about inclusion.

Always **assume less and** *always* **ask more.**

Courage

by Bhanu Jadeja-Mahal

My name is Bhanu Jadeja-Mahal, and I am the daughter of British Army officer Viraji Jethaji Jadeja, of Jamnagar. I come from a Rajput family (princely family) in India. However, I was born and bred in Mombasa, Kenya, and moved to the UK in November 1973. My partner was still studying in Nairobi, and hoped to join me later. (He did end up coming to the UK but wanted nothing to do with me or my child.)

I found accommodation in Bath with my sister and her family. However, it did not work out as planned, as they were abusive towards me. I could not defend myself as I was pregnant at the time. I then found work in the Keynsham Chocolate Factory in Bristol, but my sister's relatives took all my money and then threw me out of the house.

I spent several nights sleeping rough in the park, even trying to end my life by jumping into the river but was stopped and helped by a kind woman. She saw my bump and asked me where the father was. "In Kenya," I replied. She advised me to go to the police, as they would be able to help me. My heart started pumping fast as I said, "No, I can't, I just can't."

I just kept quiet and decided to go back to work. As I entered the factory, my supervisor said, "Look at your hair! What happened to you, Bhanu?" I explained everything and she took me to the welfare office and at last, I got the help I needed. I was offered a place in the local vicarage until I passed all the medical tests for the mother and baby home. I then got a place at a mother and baby home in Bristol and delivered a healthy, bouncy baby girl.

I then moved to Leicester and applied for a job in the police service, starting as a traffic warden. At last, I was able to provide for my daughter. I was a single mum determined to work hard and serve the community. I spoke nine languages and could read and write in all of them. This talent took me far in my job and a multicultural city such as Leicester.

I have played an important role in the police force in Leicester since April 1975 and am still working now. In 1992, I was promoted to the position of Local Support Team Officer, taking all jobs that came through the front office. At the same time, I bought my own house and I educated my daughter right up until she completed her master's degree with distinction!

I loved travelling around the world, cooking and exploring all sorts of international dishes. In 2005, I received a visit from Upkar Singh Mahal, who was a friend of my brother's.

What a surprise it was to see him after 36 years! He visited us in Leicester and we kept in touch. Six months later, we got married and honeymooned, travelling to California. Upkar introduced his friend Harjinder to my daughter and they got married in November 2009.

I took up a challenge because my mission was to give back to Leicester; the city that had given me a home and where I had brought up my daughter. I decided to volunteer for various causes.

Warning Zone is a Leicester-based charity dedicated to teaching life skills and safeguarding children. I volunteer for Education by Experience, which looks after children age 9 to 11 years old.

I also volunteer for the Youth Offending Team in Leicester on behalf of the council, which caters for teenagers aged 12 to 17.

I volunteer for the Peace Programme. This is a rehabilitation programme organised by the United Nations for prisoners and ex-offenders.

And last but not least, I help out at the Sai Baba Temple in Leicester offering Disclosure and Barring Service (DBS) awareness to help employers make safer recruitment decisions when the vulnerable or children are involved.

I wanted to run my own public speaking class but was unable to do so because many of my elder family members passed away.

In April 2022, I lost my husband after a prolonged battle with leukaemia. This has turned my life upside down. I have since joined Jamila's Legacy, a mental well-being charity in Leicester. I am also currently having physio after being injured in a bus accident.

In early December 2022, my father-in-law was admitted to hospital; I had to travel to and from the hospital daily. He passed away on 13th December at the age of 98 years.

This is my message to the world: I broke all the Asian rules!

- I was a single mum who stood up to situations and institutions.

- I educated my daughter to master's degree level.

- I worked in the police force as one of the pioneers in community support.

- I got married after the age of 50.

- I supported (and still do) my immediate and extended family in all situations.

- I supported my community in Leicester as much as I could and still volunteer as much as I can.

I hope to meet our King one day as I am 75 years old and have been serving His Majesty's Police Force for almost 48 years! But what is age? It's how young you feel!

The main force that has got me through my life is courage: the courage to leave my native country, the courage to be a single mum, the courage to educate my daughter to the highest of standards, the courage to take a job in a very male-orientated workforce in the 1970s, the courage to take chance on love in my fifties, the courage to support children and teenagers at difficult points in their lives. That is what being a bias breaker is all about.

It's All About Family

by Pam Case

*"It is not our differences that divide us.
It is our inability to recognise, accept,
and celebrate those differences."*

*Audre Lorde
American writer, radical feminist,
professor, and civil rights activist*

*"It is our inability or unwillingness to understand our
differences that keep us in fear of crossing perceived divides –
thus stifling many opportunities for acts of love and kindness."*
Pam Case

My teenage world was not the happiest place, but it was probably the whitest.

1970s Britain. A world of ultra-processed sustenance in tins and packets – from luncheon meat to instant mashed potatoes. A world where anything outside of pie, fish and chips or a Sunday roast might be proclaimed, by my mother, to be "foreign muck". Not even pizza or yoghurt graced the shelves of our fridge. I could only stare in curiosity at those dreadful freeze-dried curries as I was hurried past the supermarket shelves.

The streets of my suburb were awash with platform shoes, impossibly wide bell-bottomed jeans, fly-away shirt collars and tank tops. But at what point in my life I became aware that white was not the only colour, I do not know. Enoch Powell had already made his historic and terrible 'Rivers of Blood' speech back in 1968 but, being only five years old at the time, race had not entered my suburb or my consciousness.

You can't have an opinion on something you're not aware of.

In fact, I didn't voice many opinions on anything. An overly strict force in the shape of my mother saw to that. Even saying the word "No" could earn me repeated clouts from the palm of her hand across my bare legs. Sometimes I would be wondering what on EARTH I had said wrong on the days when she refused to speak to me or look at me. "Sent to Coventry", I would get on my knees and beg for her explanation so that I might mould myself into the type of little girl a mother could actually love, and for her forgiveness for… I knew not what.

Mum was, of course, allowed to have plenty of opinions, and she gave me the full 'benefit' of it. "You're useless. Do you hear me? I didn't want you; you weren't planned. The very fact that you were born ruined my life! Can you see the ultra-microscopic shit under my smallest fingernail? You can't – because it would take a very powerful microscope to see THAT. Let me tell you now that there's more goodness in that tiny amount of shit, not visible to the human eye, than there is in the whole of your being, or ever will be."

And on... and on...

When I reached my teens the narrative segued into "I'll kill you, so help me God, I'll bloody kill you!" and "You're going to come home here one day and find all your belongings in that front garden and the locks changed and you'll be finding somewhere else to live."

Well... there's no parenting manual, I guess.

Dad cowered away from her and simply told me to do the same. *Small wonder*, I kept myself to myself. Buried my head in books and schoolwork. Speaking of which – the lesson I loved best was French. Wow – was I fascinated by foreign languages!

We didn't "go abroad". It wasn't what working-class families did back then. I grew up viewing foreign lands and peoples through the family television. Marvelling at the lilt and pattern of other languages, whilst the irrepressible empath in me often hurt and cried at injustices of wars, famines and natural disasters. My heart went out to total strangers – victims of both past and present horrors.

Enter the curry house

Or rather… I entered the curry house. My mother, who had passed away suddenly when I was just 19, would have been horrified. "Foreign muck" became my food of choice and, to my utter delight, a kind and patient member of the management there taught me my first words of Hindi and Bengali.

Maybe that's where it all began…

I stowed those first few words and phrases away in my memory as I do with most translations I'm given. During one particular hospital stay, the lovely woman in the bed next to me swapped some of her Zulu language for some of the words I knew in Arabic. She was, she said, wanting to surprise an Arabic-speaking pal of hers. I still remember what she taught me over 20 years later. That, and the fact that we laughed so loud and long that the ward matron had severe words with us for being a disturbance of the peace.

I had also begun to travel a little. The usual Mediterranean places for British holidaymakers, then North Africa, Malaysia, Vietnam… But nowhere I ever visited called me back several times as did…

India

Wherever I go, I like to do a little research first. I want to know not only what there is to see and experience, but what is expected of ME. For example – what modes of dress, gestures, and behaviours, could be misinterpreted or cause offence? Many travellers will say to me, "Hey, why should I change MY culture to fit in?" but my reply is that causing offence is NOT my culture and I care about other people and their sensibilities – and I refuse to change my stance on that.

And so it was that I found myself, eventually, in the middle of a little fishing village in South India, with a gaggle of little kids, fascinated by my paleness and my "golden hair", following me around. I could go into the superfluous detail of how my partner and I got invited into a local family's house – but hey, there's a word limit on this chapter and suffice to say that that's what happened.

House?

Growing up, even in a working-class home, we had a brick shed as big as this family's home. Let's call it a one-storey, three-roomed hut, windowless apart from one room which had two unglazed square apertures. One of the rooms was a kitchen of sorts. Rudimentary shelving held pots and pans, and a burner on a stone slab served as a cooker.

That left two rooms, one being the parental bedroom and the other housing a couple of single beds, a cupboard and a table, and being the sleeping place for the three offspring – by now in their teens and twenties.

If you're wondering where the bathroom was – you won't guess, because it was non-existent. The only running water came from a village standpipe, and the nearby brackish river provided both bathing and laundry facilities. Ask for the toilet and you would be directed to a rickety screen of dried palm leaves at the side of the house, behind which you would tumble down the hole in the ground in the hours of darkness without the use of a torch.

I admired the resourcefulness of the wall art made from old matchboxes pinned into a pattern, and the makeshift ceiling of flattened cardboard boxes.

What else are you supposed to do when just one member of the family had work, bringing home the equivalent of around £25 per month, when the monsoon would bring that employment to a halt, and with it the only source of income that could pay for food?

Did something happen "on the spiritual plane" that day as I walked through the tattered curtain that covered the doorway?

I don't know but I do know this… that family entered my heart and soul in an instant and I knew I loved them. 'Agape', that's what it's called. Agape is almost always used to describe the love that is of and from God, whose very nature is love itself. There is no other way to describe it.

All subsequent correspondence from the UK asking what we might send over to the family was met with protestations. Eventually, the one boy, who at 19 could speak some English, caved in and requested a baseball cap and some fine felt pens.

I must point out that handwritten letters were an absolute necessity. There was but one phone in the village and someone got a TV at one point – to have the neighbours cramming into every corner of their house to get their viewing quota in. I also record here the request for cap and pens to illustrate how little the family wanted or expected from us.

Eventually, our 19-year-old correspondent reached 21 and I saw my chance. I slipped £25 into an envelope with a note to the effect that he was not allowed to protest because in our culture, 21 was a significant birthday and hadn't we accepted and participated in his culture on our visit to India? Such was the sanguine nature of all his letters thus far, he had omitted to let me know that his sister was seriously ill and there was no money to pay the hospital to cure her of pneumonia. My lad (to whom I now refer as my 'little brother') hot-footed it to the money changer and then on to pay the doctors. There's a distinct possibility that it saved her life.

Time marched on. The box of 'letters from India' I kept was added to regularly. Then, one day, the postman delivered a missive that I couldn't immediately add to the growing pile.

It required action!

I'll never forget the name Sunil, for a man bearing that name it was, who entered the fishing village with greed and ruthlessness in his heart, and evil deception on his lips. He would, he falsely promised, guarantee work for the older son of my family in a Maldivian hotel. All he would need the young man to do was purchase a return flight to the Maldives to attend an interview and to bring a substantial amount of cash for a work permit.

Being a tight-knit community in my village (yes, that's how I have come to refer to it), the neighbours rallied around and loaned my family what gold jewellery they owned, to raise the necessary cash from the local pawnbroker. Once our boy had the job and the salary to send home, the pawnbroker could be repaid, the jewellery returned, and after that – another steady income for his parents and siblings.

Except that it just didn't work like that.

Kept in a hut in the blazing Maldivian heat for three days with nothing but a little boiled tuna to eat and nothing to drink, to eventually be told that no such job or interview existed, our boy asked for his work permit payment to be reimbursed. The response? "If you want to see your own country again, you will stop asking and shut your face!"

Bundled onto the return flight and having to carry baggage for weary travellers, he earned enough rupees for the long bus journey home, and fell, exhausted and starving, through the curtain that served as a daytime doorway to his home.

"I'm so sorry for this bad news. I just don't know who else I can tell. We are the unluckiest family in the village, and we don't know what to do. The neighbours are wanting their jewellery back. What is going to happen to us? Please pray!"

Pray? No request for money. Nothing.

But I prayed all right. Over the envelope into which I had sealed £50 and a note: "I know you are hungry, and I know the neighbours want their jewellery back but PLEASE trust me – do not spend this on food or take it to the pawnbroker – just trust me." I went on to describe a certain craft I had seen in the local villages. Something I had never seen in the UK. The cost? Around 50p each. I wanted £50 worth and if I got them, I would help.

"Please God – if you're listening. Protect this envelope; no one in that village has a bank account. I have to trust you to not allow this money to be intercepted and stolen."

The day £50 worth of those crafts was thrust into my hands by the postman, I was both elated and nervous. What if no one LIKED them? My fears were unfounded. "Let's have a look then," demanded one of the girls in the office. With a shrug, I shook the envelope of dried skeleton pipal leaves out onto my own desk. "WOW!" my friend Annie exclaimed, as the beautiful oil paintings on them tumbled out and spread across my work area. Her exclamation and the way in which she dived into the pile attracted a small crowd. Before I knew it, money was raining down onto my desk and the stash of crafts had all but disappeared!

Annie and I stared at each other in amazement then started to laugh. "Hey! Let's make a spreadsheet! I'll do it!" offered Annie, ever the pragmatist. In minutes, she had organised my whole approach, telling me how much money to send back to India for the pawnbroker, how much to invest in frames for the remaining pieces, how many more leaf pictures to request, and what to charge for the framed versions. I'll always be grateful for her amazing support.

And thus… we proceeded. We sold our pictures at the back of churches, at house parties, etc. We added the beautiful kulfi pots saved for me by my friend Asit (he of the restaurant and the first words in Hindi and Bengali) and filled them with candles and potpourri. My Indian 'little brother' even started to send solid silver foot chains at a fraction of the cost of those we could buy in the UK – and they went down a storm.

In a matter of months, we had paid off the debt to the pawnbroker, the villagers had their jewellery returned, and we had booked a flight with a large bag full of the items our family had listed as 'wants'. Soap, toothpaste, perfume, shampoo, and so on.

Annie and her husband came along and, after one too many Kingfisher beers had pushed their soothing fingers down our throats, we had agreed on round two. Do it all over again, bring my 'little brother' over to the UK, get him through some qualifications, and send him back with the means of getting a better job.

I won't bore you with the details as you've read how we did it the first time. Rinse and repeat. The red tape for getting that boy to the UK was a phenomenal neck ache, but was it worth it? Judge for yourself. The trip, the qualifications, and the CV we helped our boy to write, all secured him a good job at a fairly low level. Most importantly, we had shown him what was possible. Repeated 'Employee of the Month' awards and subsequent promotions later... he is now a director of a large and prestigious operation and has insisted on repaying us with visits and gifts and looking after us on trips to India. NONE of which is necessary to us – just important to him.

But I'm getting ahead of myself.

Let's go back to when I returned to that village after clearing the debt. Everyone in the village came together to provide chairs, a table and a homecoming feast but here's the MAIN thing... Amma (which means mum) came running from that hut, with tears streaming down her beautiful face. She wet my face in turn with them and she embraced me and kissed me. She held me in one arm as she cooked for me with the other.

LOVE surpassed language, religion, culture and tradition.

I was welcomed into a family. I was mothered in a beautiful way. At last. Revisit the beginning of this chapter if you have forgotten the significance of this.

Exhausted by the effort and not wanting to feel judged for "bragging about what I did," I buried this story for many years, until fairly recently. For the umpteenth time, I had been asked, "Why do you speak Hindi?" and since I was in the comfort zone of a small group of women I knew well, I drew a deep breath and began.

The response?

"This story needs to be told! It should inspire OTHER people to reach out across perceived cultural and religious barriers. After all, it's not about what you did for them, it's equally about what it did for YOU...

It's all about family!"

The hairs on my arms stood on end. It was the moment I knew that everything had led me to this time. I am a trained presenter who loves public speaking. I love motivating others and I have always believed that THE WORLD IS A FAMILY. As such, we need to reach out to understand each other. Understanding drives out fear and promotes tolerance. The real story of the British Empire should be taught in our schools in order to educate everyone as to why Britain is a wonderfully multicultural place today.

My story demonstrates how reaching out in understanding and tolerance – and that extends to genders, abilities, ages, and so on – can make a difference, not just to others but to ourselves.

Dear family, there is so much pleasure and importance in learning and in turning that love in action.

I often use my social media presence to bring together people who are on the same mission to promote peace. I recommend great books from which we can all draw some amazing learning, understanding and tolerance. To name a few...

They: What Muslims and Non-Muslims Get Wrong About Each Other (Sarfraz Manzoor)

Empireland: How Imperialism Has Shaped Modern Britain (Sathnam Sanghera)

Brown Girl Like Me (Jaspreet Kaur)

Anglo-Indians Abroad (Dr Andrea Malam BEM)

The Power of Privilege: How White People Can Challenge Racism (June Sarpong)

The Good Immigrant (Nikesh Shukla)

It's scary being out there trying to explain things to those whose hearts are filled with bias and educated only by the one-sided "Tommy Robinson" type rhetoric. I am open to backlash from all sides. Even some people of colour have said, "White people should not talk about racism" and "Just another white woman making it all about herself." They're wrong. If all those biased people will only listen to people of their own colour – then it's going to take people like me to bridge the gap and reach into their hearts. Besides, as Jesus said, "He who is for us, cannot be against us."

Rosa Parks brought about change by sitting down. We can all stand up – for people like her.

Stories and Representation

by Alaska Harrison

*"If you are always trying to be normal
you will never know how amazing you can be."*
Maya Angelou

The first time I received a death threat, I was 12 years old.

It was early December 2007, and I was on my way to German class. Excited by the upcoming winter break, I had a spring in my step and my head in the clouds. School was something I enjoyed, I wasn't a high achiever academically or the teacher's favourite, but the escape it provided from the monotony of a semi-restrictive home life and abuse from my extended family pushed me towards education as a means to escape. It took me a while to adjust to an all-girls' school and then longer to find any friends. I was an average student but a keen participant; to this day, I still hold the record for the most clubs, societies and posts of responsibility created and/or held as a singular member. The badges would run down the entire length of my uniform lapels, clanking together when I moved at speed. As I approached my classroom, another student waved me down to give me a Christmas card.

Students piled into class after me as I sat down, card in hand, rucksack slacking on the floor. I opened the envelope excitedly and took out the card. I always loved handwritten letters and felt very lonely at the time, so a token of care and friendship, even as small as this, was something I welcomed with open arms and a beaming smile. It had an adorable orange tabby cat sitting on top of a festive-themed vintage fireplace adorned with tinsel, presents and candles and gifts which surrounded them. Surprisingly, however, upon opening it, the card was blank – it was, however, not empty.

I held it up, and from my peripheral vision saw various forms of flattened mass fall out and scatter around my desk. Confused, I collected all the pieces that had fallen on the floor, assuming it was just bad glue/crafting materials but I was wrong; it was magazine cuttings of words, jaggedly cut out similar to a ransom note, words like 'You' 'will' 'hang' 'death' 'Kill' and 'black'.

I was born and raised in South London. My mother had me when she was young, and to keep me safe we had to move away from her mother's house in Wandsworth and would visit my aunts and grandmothers on occasion when time and work inevitably got in the way. She was always working out of necessity; I have fond memories of waking up at 5 a.m., my mother coming through the door after a long shift working the bar at a central London club, with a McDonald's breakfast in tow. She'd force herself to stay awake just so she could be with me during my meal whilst cuddling me. To be blunt, my mother is a force of nature, my hero. Born into a large family with seven other siblings she raised me alone and worked hard to give me everything I needed. We lived in a small two-bedroomed flat on the sixth floor of a council estate in Roehampton built in the 1920s, where I spent the entirety of my childhood.

I learnt earlier than most that intent doesn't equal or negate impact, with white people constantly critiquing, commenting and touching my body and hair without asking permission, students and colleagues yelling at me in hallways about how I must be albino, calling me a freak for existing in the body I was born into because I didn't look how they *thought* biracial people should look. Whilst my lighter skin was amenable to them, my body shape, curly hair, wide nose and full lips were unacceptable. There was no day-to-day discussion on anti-racism, and terms like "microaggression" were a distant unknown to me; when you don't even possess access to the language needed to understand something, it's almost impossible to quantify and reflect on as an individual.

Months later, aged 13, I couldn't take it anymore. I rushed home from school sobbing uncontrollably. When my mum finally convinced me to tell her what was wrong, it seemed to fall out of me violently: "I just wish I was white... why can't I just be *normal* like you?" I stared at my shoes as my tears fell onto the floor, never daring to look at her as I said it. I felt so ashamed, so guilty for the crime of existing, just – embarrassed.

I received more death threats and regular racial abuse from colleagues at work, friends, family and even schoolmates from primary school all the way into university and beyond. Even with this seemingly constant trauma, I still walked through the world with a level of light-skinned white privilege that will always exist with me on some level. Even if I wasn't cognizant of it at the time, it was always there. I used to methodically straighten my hair in order to 'pass', allowing people to think I was white for many years as a younger teen because it seemed easier... safer. Even though it physically damaged me doing it and drove a huge psychological wedge between myself and many who loved me, the ability to do so was in itself an admission of white supremacy. Without "the talk" from my family or any kind of discussion on similar topics throughout my education, I wasn't prepared for any of it.

My father and I had just begun to really connect and were finally building a relationship together. I was 18 and recovering from various mental health crises after a sexual assault and suicide attempt, when I was notified of his deportation court date. He is just another father caught at the beginning of what is now, in 2023, a 13-year-and-counting national crisis from the creation and implication of the UK's Hostile Environment Policies.

I've always loved movies. We lived in working poverty with my mother working multiple jobs to keep up with basic living costs and bills, so I grew up mostly watching her old VHS tapes, and uncountable hours' worth of eighties movies ignited my passion for media. I also read everything I could; these stories are what gave me structure, and displayed models of living I would integrate into my own psyche. This was how I learned to make sense of the world and my place in it.

Meeting my grandmother on my father's side for the first time and being introduced to the TV series *Roots* (1977) are two of the most significant moments of my life.

I started researching all I could after that, upon discovering the origin of race came from a single book, the biography of Prince Henry the Navigator, written in 15th century Portugal by Gomes de Zurara. I was shocked this wasn't taught to me in school. It made me wonder what else I hadn't been taught. This was the source material many in history and modern society would subsequently draw from as they created the idea of a monolithic group of people based solely on race despite the fact that people from the global majority have extremely specific and separate cultural identities, history, traditions and people. This book would go on to be used as "proof" that all people with Black African heritage are inherently lesser than the "superior" European/Caucasian individual. This single biography, commissioned by the Prince himself, created a false but imposed justification for enslaving African people. I became aware of how important stories can be, and since then, never stopped searching or reading.

I was standing at the entrance to the court, trying to self-soothe by pulsing my fingertips against my palm when it hit me; this was a real-life deportation hearing; it was nothing like the movies, there was no maverick renegade lawyer to magically appear and fix everything, the system just isn't designed for that. With many working in immigration law overworked and underpaid, we were not special, just another case, just another day. I was called into the hearing and stood up in front of the tribunal staff, choking down tears the moment I was asked to speak. They remarked on the supporting evidence I'd submitted, an impact letter I had written and rewritten. To this day, with all the professional writing I have completed, I have never redrafted something so many times. But it did not matter; this was an immigration tribunal, not a movie.

Growing up as the only queer non-white person in a white heteronormative family was a struggle, to say the least. Amongst my mother's side of the family (whom I grew up with), women weren't upheld and celebrated in the same way the men were; misogyny, racism and homophobia seemed to be our only family pastime. I have many memories of being questioned and interrogated by my uncles about how feminism was 'ridiculous', racism doesn't exist in the UK, and homosexuality was inherently wrong. Sometimes outright and other times implied through jokes and slurs, I knew in my heart I was right, but I was barely 10 years old in 2005, not exactly a prime position to be in to debate and push back on hateful ideas held by a lot of the adults around me.

They didn't realise, of course, at the time the long-term effects their actions would have. Even innocuous actions I now know have negatively affected my ability to live, as well as how I have developed into who I am today, good and bad.

It is incredibly important to note, that with over 40% of the UK population having a single adverse childhood experience as it pertains to ACE markers, and over 8% experiencing four or more, I am by no means an outlier.

Adverse Childhood Experiences (ACEs) are "highly stressful, and potentially traumatic, events or situations that occur during childhood and/or adolescence. They can be a single event or prolonged threats to, and breaches of, the young person's safety, security, trust or bodily integrity." (Young Minds, 2018)

When every single part of you, the core of what makes you up, is constantly questioned, denigrated, dismissed and humiliated, you eventually develop a deep sense of inadequacy, dissociation and loneliness. My grandfather, for example, would use me as what I can only describe as a 'fidget toy'; he'd tell stories in the kitchen whilst I stood there beside him and he twirled my hair as he told other adults stories. He never once asked for permission and never did the same with anyone else in the family, despite having many other cousins regularly around/visiting. It seems like something trivial in comparison to everything else I've been through, but as an adult, I now know it contributed heavily to a feeling of my body being for others and not myself. When you learn from a young age that you specifically aren't allowed bodily autonomy in the same way others are, it makes it difficult to then feel empowered with issues of consent and autonomy. I learnt at nine years old that I am only palatable and my body only agreeable if I am a piece of entertainment for someone else.

There were periods of time, of course, where friends and extended family did embrace a temporary interest in Black culture, but it was always for their own entertainment or social advantage. They would adopt 'blaccents' and take up rapping in their spare time, whilst openly saying racial slurs around me, suddenly dressing as if they weren't living in/from a white suburb in Surrey because for them it was just a phase, a time period of experimentation. I don't think they understand to this day how damaging it was to see and hear that growing up when the only access to/reflection of my culture I was supplied with, was offensive stereotypes, shallow bastardisations, misappropriation and most of the time, total falsehoods.

After three suicide attempts, being subjected to multiple assaults by people whom I thought I could trust, and years of therapy, I can only now at 27 reflect on my past as a large reason I am who I am today. But isn't that always the way with hindsight?

I needed advocacy, someone to stand up and say, "This isn't right." Whilst my mum protected me as best she could and I was always happy when I was with her, she ultimately couldn't always be around. We were just one of millions of other families in a similar position at the time and this has only got worse in 2023. Out of those living through poverty in the UK, six out of every ten are in working poverty; that is, households who have at least one working adult in employment but due to low wages, bad working conditions and lack of employee support, still find themselves unable to afford basic household expenses, living from pay cheque to pay cheque.

> *"The past is what makes the present coherent,*
> *and the past will remain horrible for*
> *exactly as long as we refuse to assess it honestly."*
> *James Baldwin (Dark Days)*

It wasn't until my early twenties that I finally saw someone that looked like me. I remember watching the television and a woman appeared as if from the ether, her familiar wide features seemingly cutting through the screen. I knew I was alone yet looked around the room for a witness, to check it wasn't some sick joke or trick, to check I wasn't dreaming – my shock wore off and I burst into guttural tears. I have yet to have a moment of total release like that to this day; it was like the first breath you take after nearly drowning. In a matter of seconds, it changed something inside me. Her smile was so wide, I spent the rest of the day imagining her doing everyday tasks like walking her dog, grocery shopping and going over work with colleagues. It meant I wasn't wrong. My existence and personhood **weren't** incorrect. If this woman on television existed, it meant I could as well.

Stories are one of our most important resources. I believe that it is integral to be able to share with each other our truths and histories in order to take the necessary steps to heal as individuals and as a society. Representation, equity and truth are just the beginning and bringing these into my career has been beyond fulfilling. Though I am currently employed primarily as a writer, I've worked across many of the creative industries with a strong pull towards comedy as a vehicle for change. I am now studying to go into Museum Curation to explore these passions further, whilst discovering and presenting lost, forgotten and hidden history with a focus on minoritized communities.

From the moment I was born, my life has always been interrupted and steered by governmental policies and societal opinions, from the healthcare I struggled to receive because of my gender and ethnicity, to losing the only home

I knew due to the 2013 "Bedroom Tax". As I wanted to go to university, this meant my old bedroom would now be seen as a spare room whilst I was away studying, increasing costs and forcing my mother to move.

Statistically, I shouldn't be in my current position. Statistically, I should probably not be alive. Many similar to me won't ever be given even half the opportunities I have had in the past, because, to be blunt – how can you be successful if you cannot survive?

> *"There are no sidelines, we are all in it.*
> *We are implicated and if I'm not joining the struggle*
> *to dismantle a system that advantages me – I am complicit."*
> *John Biewen*
> *'Seeing White' TEDx talk*

The Power of Being "The Black Sheep" of the Family

by Zishan Khan

My name is Zishan Khan. I am a visionary, creative and a dream chaser, who has gained a wealth of knowledge in entrepreneurship, sales and personal development over the years through self-education and working in the corporate world. My vision/mission is to empower millions of young people to become their own boss, and live their life by their own design, by awakening their minds to the greatness that resides within them.

We've all been in situations where we feel a bit out of place, have felt misunderstood, or maybe even unwanted.

When people feel left out or rejected, many turn to the understanding of their families for comfort. However, people who identify as "the black sheep of the family" have a different experience of rejection and misunderstanding. For that reason, it can be extremely difficult when you're the "black sheep" as the people making you feel excluded are your own family members.

This was my experience in my teens. I come from a mixed family; my dad is from Bangladesh and my mum is from Pakistan. So, two different languages and cultures had to find common ground in our house. I am the eldest of four, and coming from an Asian family brings its own weight of expectations and obligations – I was subjected to all of them.

Being in my teen in the nineties, music played a big part in my life. At the age of 16, I was hanging out with musicians, producers, gig organisers and venues. Being creative, I taught myself how to play guitar and bass, and started a few bands of my own and joined others. By the time I was 19, I was organising gigs for venues, booking our band and other bands to play there.

This sounds like so much fun, right? It was when I was in that atmosphere and outside the house. However, as soon as I got home, I was a different Zishan. A Zishan with obligations to attain the standards put up by my dad. When I announced at home what my passion and joy were and what I wanted to pursue, I was met with countless resistance from my dad. As no one has ever been a musician in our families ever, it was something looked down upon as well as being thought of as not stable enough to earn a good salary and live a decent life.

I was living a double life from the age of 16, being the black sheep of the family. This took a lot out of me. This double lifestyle stayed with me once I left home and lived on my own, as it was now ingrained in me. I had amazing music-based roles in my twenties but now work in the corporate world. This too has taken its toll on me as I parked my passion for music and focused on my corporate career.

Being the black sheep of the family, I was still doing things that were not acceptable in our family. I was not an accountant, I was not a doctor, I was not even an engineer.

The rebel in me decided I would still do what made me happy so I decided to work for a pizza place, taking orders over the phone as my very first job at the age of 17. What I had set in motion here without realisation was my path of self-discovery, breaking the family bias creating the power in being the black sheep of the family.

On the path to the power of being the black sheep

I am one of those crazy people you meet that enjoys everything they do, who always has a grin on their face – sometimes they are very loud and sometimes quiet. I believe it came from a positive outlook on life and being optimistic about anything and everything. It was not always like this; as mentioned earlier, I had lots of resistance from my dad in wanting to do what I wanted. I believe this made me create the life I wanted to live and be happy with, and it came in the form of living a double life. I am a firm believer that if you are looking for something and it doesn't exist, then you need to create it. In my teens, it came in the form of creating this double life: living it large in my music world creating amazing music and friendships, whilst also respecting my home life, and never mixing the two.

This continued in my working life at the pizza place. I was a junior, handling calls and taking delivery orders over the phone. Being a quick learner and open to opportunities, I was promoted to supervisor within seven months. This was my first taste of achievement and success. I saw it as appreciation and being recognised for what I was worth and could bring to the table. This opened me up to possibilities of what else I could achieve. I moved into tech retail, starting as a sales rep for a reputable brand. My double life, which I had created for my dad and family, was now here with me at work, as I looked at much an authority figure as my dad and showed my best self. It was great and it helped me move up the ladder and into the corporate world, managing clients and their sales teams.

The reason I mention all this is because I was told I would not amount to anything from my dad and that I would have a hard life, as I was not following the pre-destined path that he and the rest of the family were on. That first promotion made me realise that I could take a different path yet achieve similar results, and on my own terms.

In all my workplaces and roles, I gave 110% and really enjoyed it. Looking back, I believe the continuous learning mindset kept it interesting. Of course, there were ups and down and it wasn't plain sailing, but I was always ready for what was next. I still say this to myself now, "It's just for now, and tomorrow it won't matter as there will be something else."

Are you an introvert or an extrovert?

It's a question everyone's been asked at some point in their lives, one which I believe carries a lot of weight.

I was never able to answer this question. I was neither! I enjoyed being out and about, but also enjoyed being alone. It was never one thing or the other – I was happy in both. I didn't need a quiet place to recharge myself or to be at social events to thrive. I somehow was able to balance both worlds and give equal attention to them. I also believe this is the power of being the black sheep; I learned early on in life by living the double life. I had an extroverted life with my friends and my creative life, where I would be performing on stage with the band and running around, and then in the next breath would come off the stage and be sitting quietly with my drink. You would never have been able to tell that I had been on stage earlier, performing excitedly.

This has given me the power to balance the flow of adult life, by being an **ambivert**.

Some of the signs to look for if you're an ambivert are:

- Being a good listener and communicator.

- Able to adjust to the person or situation.

- Feeling comfortable in social settings, but also valuing your 'alone' time.

- Able to provide balance.

How are you always smiling?

I am asked this question all the time. I never knew how to respond to it and laughed it off. I believe the world is a mirror and you only see what you are projecting out there. It's not to say that I didn't have any challenges or obstacles. I had my fair share and more as I had two different lives, so twice the heartbreaks, disappointments, let-downs, setbacks; you name it, I endured it.

I started to ask this question to myself: Why do I always keep smiling?

Today, smiling happens very naturally but here is what I think happened when I began on the path of creating the power of being the black sheep of the family.

Accepting what is: Whatever I do and however frustrated I become, I cannot change what already is. Accepting what already 'is' in a wholehearted manner and trying to shape the future into what I want it to be, helps me be at ease with the present conditions and take the next step forward, rather than complaining. I cannot help the past or what already 'is'.

Responding and not reacting: Most of our actions in today's busy world, where everyone is trying to run as fast as they can, are reactions rather than responses. When our reactions lead to unpleasant consequences, we wish we could go back and change the way we handled the situation. Anger and frustration destroy us more than the person/situation we are angry about. When I get angry or frustrated and destroy my own peace, then the cause of the frustration has definitely succeeded! When I maintain my cool, again by accepting what has happened and take a moment to think and respond, I am more confident about my actions and the regret rate is sure to go down.

Enjoying the little things: Almost all the time we have something going on in our heads and we rarely pay attention to the little things in our lives. Enjoying an early morning or evening walk, a random conversation with a stranger, getting wet in the rain, gazing at the stars, or a hug from a friend: the list of beautiful things around us is endless. But we rarely stop for a moment to pay proper attention to them and enjoy them. Actually, a large part of our lives is all these little things put together and it is important to enjoy them.

Spreading some love: I am not saying we should be lovey-dovey all the time. But spreading some love around keeps us peaceful within. A few words of sincere appreciation or apology, a few hugs and smiles a day or, even better, bringing a smile to someone else's face. And trust me, we are not doing anyone a favour but ourselves. On a busy and frustrating day, running into a smiling face seems to magically ease all the frustration and automatically brings a smile to my face. Who wouldn't want to live in a happy world? But to receive something, we need to give something. So, spread some love and smiles and get some back.

These little things I inculcated helped me keep the world inside and outside me pleasant. When all is good inside and outside, we smile even more. And that is why I keep smiling all the time.

I would love to add that it does not mean I do not have problems in life. It is just that I face them with a smile. Every so often, I have my moments of depression and sadness and want to cry my heart out, but I smile again before you even know I cried.

How are you so calm?

This was another question I had no answer for. I was calm in extreme stress and suffering situations. Soon I started asking myself the same question: Why am I so calm when others are stressed?

Leading the double life for my dad, I would often find myself instinctively distancing myself from where the troubles were concentrated, subconsciously analysing where the situation was heading and positioning myself accordingly. Indeed, if I was good at anything, it was positioning myself.

I realise that this instinctive behaviour would spread across other areas of my life where it is most needed. We make a lot of decisions on a daily basis, most of which are mundane and trivial. However, some are pivotal to how our future will unfold.

Positioning myself would look like this:

- I keep my expectations in check.
- I take responsibility for my actions.
- I embrace the Joy of Missing Out.
- I set healthy boundaries.
- I surround myself with supportive people.

I don't know if you noticed that I was doing a lot of things from mindset, habit creating, being disciplined with myself, and being open to whatever came my way. I was doing all this without knowing that I was doing this. All I knew was I was the black sheep of the family and I had to create my path and keep moving forward with each and every new day. I always looked at life differently to the norm out there. For me, everything is possible and we are the only ones blocking ourselves.

Imagine if I had proper guidance or resources in my teens to understand what I set upon creating, and been shown possibilities via best practices of creating even better habits, mindset and discipline. I am not saying that I am not happy with where I am now, but only stating that I could have been an even better version of who I am today.

This is why I am highly passionate about creating something for young people where they get the opportunity to explore and learn how to create a future they really want for themselves, by making conscious and informed decisions and having a clear blueprint of what that looks like.

Do you feel like the black sheep in the family? The square peg that doesn't fit in the round hole? The ideas person who constantly gets told "it's always been done this way"?

I will leave you with these questions to consider:

- Do you fully identify with being a black sheep?

- How do you cope with being the black sheep?

- What ways of being or thoughts or behaviours did you create to keep yourself safe and sane?

Remember, being the black sheep of the family means that you are strong, unique and brave! You've stuck to your guns and developed into a strong person, despite a painful family dynamic.

Start by seeing yourself as a resourceful and independent person. You need to acknowledge your strengths and gifts, and stand proud and strong in what you believe in.

As much as possible, ground yourself in the life you have built outside of the home, rather than keep trying to seek your parents' love, admiration or approval. Paradoxically, their respect may come once you have asserted yourself. When you can really see yourself for who you are and fully embrace that, you will experience a sense of calmness and compassion, and that will keep you grounded even when you have to go home and face many old triggers from your parents, siblings and relatives.

My dad accepted that I have achieved far more than he thought I would and he apologised for his behaviour over the years. Knowing what I know now and being a parent myself, I can understand where he was coming from; all he wanted was the best for me. He was only able to express it the way he knew and he did not have the vocabulary nor the mindset to understand; therefore he did his best with the tools he was handed by his family and society.

"Your future is created by what you do today, not tomorrow."
Robert Kiyosaki
American author and entrepreneur

The Queen of Empathy
by Dr Andrea Malam BEM

Did you know that everyone has or should have a vision? Be it big or small, you need one! A vision of what you do and why you do it.

My vision: A world where individuals are free to step into their courage and connect within to reveal and share their compassion, strength and wisdom for a better world.

My aim: To serve humanity and inspire others to live the life I live.

What does that really mean?

Does it mean that I am creating and building dreams with certainty?

For me, serving humanity meant I was serving the needy, the vulnerable and the underprivileged. That was a challenge. But who doesn't like a challenge? I know that it was ambitious, but I so wanted to contribute to the world by making that small mark.

I started by getting in sync with my values.

I call my top three values my 3Cs:

Courage – When we have the courage to be ourselves, without being afraid to speak up.

Connection – When we have a sense of belonging and connecting with our community.

Compassion – When we show concern and motivation to help and support others.

These values are such an important aspect of our human needs. Everything I aim to do has been purposeful, be it my career, home life, profession, or my passion.

There was a time in my life when I felt unhappy, unappreciated and unloved. The fear of being judged or feeling hurt. The thought of not being good enough. The fear of losing myself, my identity.

I began to lose who "Andrea" was.

For a long time, I felt unsettled about my identity. I was often made to feel different about who I was, my culture and my heritage. The last few years have taught me to be strong. But how strong am I?

I play an important and essential role in many lives, often under much stress, but always with a smile.

Courage comes in many forms and can inspire you to inspire others. If not now, when?

I was always called the Strong One...

The biggest challenge that I had to face in my early years was having to be the strong one, supporting others. I was always called the strong one in my family, as looking after each other was very common. And at a very young age, I faced the death of loved ones and other trauma in the family.

We make our own choices based on how we feel and the environment around us. I had a choice; to be the strong one, or to allow myself to become a victim of circumstances.

And there was no way I was going to become the victim, as I realised I could be the strong one, and from being the strong one, I could then support others too.

What really breaks my heart is seeing children and their families suffer. With my background in supporting charities and the community, I really wanted to do something to make a difference to children's lives. To do something meaningful for children who are ill, and who are suffering.

I believe that everyone needs someone in their corner, a 'strong one' in their life, helping support them to be as normal as possible, and allowing them to be a child. That matters a lot to me.

That is why I make sure children have support in the form of Care Kits bags, group outdoor visits, laptops, smartphones and the education that they have the right to, to be able to achieve.

I do not have to prove to myself that I am the strong one, but I want to be the shoulder where others can stand and grow. That is my aim.

So, whether I am working with children in schools, hospices or homes, I want them to have a safe environment and space around them, and have the best life possible in what is often a short amount of time. I want to help children everywhere – whether they are in India, the United Kingdom or elsewhere.

They need to grow up as whole as possible. That is what I want because everyone deserves a strong one on their side.

And yes, I am delighted for it to be me, but it could be you too!

My need to be myself turned into my passion and that is what led me to my purpose. I wanted my story to be the reason someone else feels they can have a dream, build on it, and then see it come true.

So, I started with setting my first goal, which was understanding who I am. Finding out who I was underneath, the Real Me, by being the person I wanted to be!

I knew I had to have a plan, because as we all know, a goal without a plan is just a wish. Reaching these goals kept me motivated. And, as the saying goes, staying motivated helps you crush more goals.

I did this by asking myself who I was, before building connections with other people. Perhaps I had been vulnerable once, but now my vulnerability became my strength. I started becoming aware of my own emotions and how they could affect those around me.

I used to be a people-pleaser and learnt a hard lesson after experiencing loss and trauma. Grief forced me to look deeper into myself, and my life.

The art of knowing myself. No one in this world can be 'you' better than you.

I became my own healer.

In the past, I had always suffered from self-doubt. I ended up letting go of many opportunities because of this, missing out on many exciting projects.

Now I faced the challenges by changing my mindset, grabbing new opportunities and developing new skills.

I then realised that by helping children and their families, I was helping my own inner self. We all have a healing power in ourselves. We just need to believe in ourselves, step into that power and tell ourselves we are worthy.

If you are looking for someone to support and encourage you to be yourself, then let that person be me. I can help you make a difference to that dream that you are hesitating to fulfil.

I wanted to make a huge difference to the lives of others by providing awareness and educating the community about the support we could provide. So began the journey of my charity, Saving Dreams (see page 161).

Saving Dreams supports communities in the United Kingdom, India and Nepal. My dream of making a difference for others was starting to become a reality. I am fulfilling my dream, walking through my life in service of others.

True Leadership

What are the best or top qualities that a Leader needs in order to inspire others?

How about Vision, Passion, Integrity, Commitment, Accountability, Confidence, Empathy and Self-Awareness?

With so much change in the world, Emotional Intelligence (EQ) is also vitally important and something we all need. It helped me become a better leader, mentor and coach. I use my knowledge of EQ to guide my thoughts and the way I think.

Emotional Intelligence is essential to your professional success too. People with good EQ have excellent leadership skills.

The core aspects of Emotional Intelligence are Self-Knowledge and Awareness, Self-Control, Self-Management, Social Skills, and last but not least, Empathy.

For me, Empathy comes first at the very top of my list. Empathy is an enormous concept. Empathy was my strength. I taught myself to be better at empathy.

If you have empathy, this is a true gift. You are far more likely to identify with other people's situations and see things from their perspective. The knowledge you gain from empathy can help you to use appropriate non-verbal communication.

This became my niche, driven by my passion, wisdom and service.

I was an Empath!

It helped me to relate to others on a basic human level with determination, trying to understand people with different opinions and voices. As an empath, we love to help and support others, so it's crucial to set boundaries for ourselves as well.

We all feel emotions – both positive and negative. We just need to regulate or manage them.

Often, when one is stuck in a rut, one doesn't realise it until one is well and truly in it. That is often when you stop dreaming big for yourself and others around you.

There is so much talk about diversity at the moment – it seems to be the 'buzz' word. However, no action gets taken! I have successfully tried to raise diversity awareness in ethnic and racial bias, and have contributed significantly across Law Enforcement and other sectors to implementing change and collaborative practices, as part of leading the various staff associations.

I had the opportunity to work in the Law Enforcement arena of the Civil Service. The Civil Service had a problem; nobody in the BAME (black, Asian and minority ethnic) community trusted or had faith in the workforce staff associations. The organisation wanted to appear inclusive to the rest of the world, yet within the structure itself, there was so much focus on ranks and grades, which highlighted subtle yet rigid hierarchies.

I used my position as a leader in diversity to define and push the boundaries, voice opinions and get opinions voiced, as well as tackle change.

As an ethnic minority woman in the Civil Service dominated by unconscious biases and many other barriers, I had to learn to be tough and build trust and connect with people with different and varied experiences from all sorts of different backgrounds. I realised that I could never give up trying to make that small difference. One never knows what is around the corner and how what you do will impact or help someone.

I help leaders become better leaders. I help them to identify the obstacles standing between them and their goals. I meet many people from different walks of life and help them change their mindsets and boundaries, which really helps with limited beliefs and taking charge of oneself. I help them to focus on the solution as well as the problem.

As a leader and role model, I have seen many failures, flaws and issues in the system. With the trust I had in myself, I was able to be confident with my "No", and clear about my "Yes".

The first question I ask clients is "What is wrong?" rather than "Are you okay?" I help them to not fear failure as everyone needs failure as a lesson that will allow them to get better. You need to recognise the signs of failure and commit to making small improvements to help yourself. This makes you a thought leader.

We cannot change the past or the present, but we can change the future. We need to focus on developing ourselves in such a way that we can be a bridge for others through diversity.

I am an ordinary woman doing extraordinary things – an honourable woman creating, building and Saving Dreams. I create a safe environment for my community to speak up with courage, compassion and connection.

When one has something one believes in, one has the motivation. I make every day an opportunity to serve others, giving them happiness and joy. What you give is what you will receive, and sometimes what you receive is more than what you give...

In 2017, I received the Queen's Medal for Long Service and Good Conduct within Law Enforcement. Shortly after, I was featured as one of 100 women highlighted in the Civil Service campaign, "100 years, 100 women, past, present and future." This thrust me into the spotlight.

Over the years, my achievements include winning various awards, such as the Women of the World Lifetime Achievement Award, Diversity Role Model Award, Admired Global Indians Award, and Outstanding Achievers Award. In addition, I gained an Honorary Doctorate in Humanities.

Last but not the least, I was awarded a British Empire Medal in the 2022 Queen's New Year's Honours List for implementing change in Diversity and Inclusion across Law Enforcement.

When you do what you love.

When you love what you do.

When you are tough and tender at the same time.

When you are proud of who you are – you are a Queen. Wear your Crown with pride.

Is that not what we tell others?

It took me years to overcome the bias, bullying, age and gender gap in Inclusion, Diversity & Equality.

Now I am a Leader, believing in myself and following my dreams.

As a multi-award-winning leader, ambassador, role model and chairperson of diversity groups, I am not afraid of challenges and breaking barriers; I call myself a BIAS BREAKER!

Meet the Authors

Archna Gohil

Archna Gohil is a strong-minded woman who can accomplish anything she sets her mind to. She encourages others to step out of the box and assists them in becoming a better version of themselves.

For many years, Archna worked in Law Enforcement, including the British Transport Police where she helped set up and launch the Ethnic Minority Network Support Group, giving a voice to those who were less able to voice their opinions. She has worked for many other organisations, always helping and supporting others. She currently works for Next Steps, a supported-living recruitment company.

With her diverse work and life experiences, she is a servant leader giving her time to others and volunteers on a regular basis.

Archna is proud of her two children, who are now at university.

Archna's purpose in life is to speak out against injustice, helping anyone and everyone.

"This is your time and place – Do it NOW."

Connect with Archna:

www.linkedin.com/in/archna-gohil-70607a39

Louise Slattery

Louise Slattery is a Clinical Hypnotherapist based in London, who specialises in Confidence Coaching. Louise transforms others who are struggling with feeling lost, by using empathy and her life experiences.

She transformed herself from someone totally lost in life, to speaking in front of huge crowds and creating coaching programs. Her signature program, "RESURRECT Your Life," has been followed by clients around the world, and she doesn't plan on stopping there! She is on a mission to transform millions of lives worldwide with her unique therapy technique, MINDspiders®.

Despite all her professional achievements, being an autism mummy is her biggest life achievement. She intends to change the way autism is perceived worldwide along with helping the autism family's mental health by setting up her new charity in 2023.

The charity is to honour her son Kieran and his siblings, Danny and Sunny, and will help families affected by autism to manage their daily lives with hypnotherapy and family support to keep families together.

Connect with Louise:

www.louiseslatterycoaching.com

www.linkedin.com/in/louise-slattery-hypno-coaching-😇-848216228

https://www.facebook.com/people/Louise-Slattery-Coaching/100086289494153/

Nirmala Bhojani

Nirmala Bhojani is a journalist and author of *Ordinary Women, Extraordinary Lives*. Nirmala came to the UK in 1986, having lived in Malawi, East Africa for six years.

Growing up in India, as the eldest child with two younger brothers, Nirmala had a BA (Hons) in English Literature and a Postgraduate qualification in Journalism and Mass Communication.

Settling in Leicester in 1987, Nirmala became a single parent while working for Leicester Libraries and the local paper, *Leicester Mercury*. Nirmala soon realised that women here faced many challenges with both work opportunities and within the Asian community.

After having set up campaigns to empower women in 1999, such as support groups for single parents and those who suffered domestic violence and abuse, Nirmala also set up the WOW (Women of the World) Awards in 2017. The campaign to #bethechange is on the WOW Woman of the World Facebook page and has 30 volunteers, who offer support to women all over the world who have suffered from domestic violence and abuse.

Nirmala is a mother of two, grandmother of four and an activist who wants a better world for all, irrespective of ability, colour, race and religion.

Nirmala was awarded the East Midlands Women's Award for services to the community in 2017.

Connect with Nirmala:

www.linkedin.com/in/nirmala-bhojani-014b71254
www.facebook.com/nirmala.bhojani
www.facebook.com/groups/2280945175496352

Jermaine Gregory

I'm a father of three children and currently live with my partner in the UK. After moving back to Birmingham from Nottingham having studied music, I got married, had my first two children, but sadly, we separated. I later moved to London in pursuit of work in the music industry.

After a stint at a professional music agency based in Canary Wharf, and a period with the Head Agent's own company, I continued with my own music agency.

I am now assisting my partner's organisation in bridging the gap between mental health and spirituality in building business relationships around the UK and the Americas.

I also coach people with a few creative project ideas on the table as well as having a podcast called Curious Anarchy, where we highlight guests from various businesses and creative backgrounds. I'll be looking to curate events and hope to start my own charitable initiative.

My one wish for the world is to be more expressive in love because love is everything and heals so much.

Connect with Jermaine:

www.linkedin.com/in/jermaine-gregory-06319b42
www.twitter.com/_CuriousAnarchy
www.instagram.com/_curiousanarchy

Dr Bijna Kotak Dasani
MBE FRSA

Bijna advises and serves the boards of various firms in the Venture Capital ecosystem across the globe. She has also led Strategy, (Digital) Transformation and Innovation within the Financial Services sector across the UK, EMEA, the Americas and Asia Pacific for over two decades.

Bijna also holds Advisory (Board) roles with the Inclusive Companies Network, FinTech Connect, CIONET, Cajigo and DMU Alumni Women's Network, and is an Ambassador for Surviving Economic Abuse (SEA), a registered UK Charity.

Additionally, she serves as a Host/Judge for a portfolio of initiatives including EfMA, the Inclusive Companies Awards, the Dublin Tech Summit and The Diversity in Tech Awards, powered by Microsoft and the Vanguard Awards (India).

Bijna is listed in Fortune India's Most Dynamic (Business) Personalities 2022 and is an appointed Member of the Most Excellent Order of the British Empire (2020) by Her Majesty Queen Elizabeth II for her services to Diversity and Inclusion in Financial Services. She has received honours from various institutions across the World over the decades for her contribution to Financial Services and also Diversity, Equity and Inclusion.

In addition to being featured in various books, publications and podcasts, Bijna is a Fellow of the Royal Society of Manufactures and Commerce (FRSA), and an alumnus of Oxford University and De Montfort University.

Connect with Dr Bijna:

www.bijna.com
www.linkedin.com/in/bijna
www.facebook.com/bijnakdasani
www.twitter.com/drbijna
www.instagram.com/thedrbijna

Kate Wilson

Kate Wilson is a career-driven mother of three girls, with a passion to break biases and influence change for future generations. At 19 years of age, Kate joined Merseyside Police and worked in various roles including the Operational Support Unit and the Robbery Team, and spent the latter half of her career specialising in financial crime, moving to the North West Regional Organised Crime Unit whilst on an operation.

Whilst pregnant with her third child, Kate obtained a MA in Financial Crime and Financial Investigation, which enabled her to transition careers into the private sector. She is now working as a Senior Cyber Crime Specialist in a global organisation.

Growing up, Kate was heavily involved in sports and found a love for netball, representing Wales at both U17 and U21 level. She continues to be a sports enthusiast and is a big supporter of promoting female athletes. Coming from a family of grafters, she prides herself on being successful at work and continues this ethos, believing work provides identity and belonging. However, she also believes that societal pressures hinder women in the workplace and impede gender parity.

Owing to her career choices, Kate has mainly worked in male-dominated environments and has experienced a vast amount of gender bias. With that said, she also thinks there is a fine balance to achieving equality, and the right person is needed for the right job regardless of gender, or any other protected characteristic.

Connect with Kate:

www.linkedin.com/in/kate-wilson-2417a5133
www.instagram.com/sheisbossingit

Emma Jones

Emma Jones is a highly regarded Senior Consultant for a leading global cybersecurity and technology company. She currently advises organisations around the world on how to enhance their ability to respond to a cyberattack.

Emma's early career was spent in the UK public sector where she latterly developed national law enforcement cyber capabilities and implemented strategies to protect the public.

In both professional and voluntary capacities, Emma continually champions diversity and works tirelessly to embed everyday inclusion. She is involved in numerous associated initiatives and has recently been recognised for her pioneering work dedicated to building inclusive cyber response teams.

*"To be intentional about inclusion,
start by always assuming less and always asking more."*

Connect with Emma:

www.linkedin.com/in/emma-jones-8356931b8

Bhanu Jadeja-Mahal

I was born in Kenya and come from a family of ten siblings seven sisters and three brothers); I am the eighth. On taking ill, my father decided to visit his family in India. He returned but passed away on my seventh birthday which was also his birthday. My mother did dressmaking to make ends meet, and we grew up in hardship, with no benefits or any help. I educated myself as a stenographer but my big brother would not let me work in Mombasa. There was a huge exodus of people leaving Uganda and Kenya, so my mother decided to move us to the UK. My partner was at Nairobi University which would help us so I made a move.

After a few months, I found I was pregnant and went through domestic abuse. I lived rough on the streets of Bath and eventually found a mother and baby home. I had a baby girl in 1974.

I joined Leicestershire Constabulary on 7th April 1975 as a Traffic Warden, pounding the streets of Leicester. Life wasn't kind – I had a heart attack at 26 years of age - but my many languages and friendly attitude, as well as some good friends, helped me out.

In 1983, I was attacked by someone and was in a coma for eight hrs. After nine weeks, I reported back on duty. Incredibly, my attacker walked past me sometime later so he was arrested.

My policing job was so important to help me bring my child up; I was inspired by my mother to bring up a child respectfully. I also helped loads of abused girls and young women; my arms were and still are open to help anyone out there.

I am a very popular figure in Leicester as a bridge between the police and the community. My senior officers believe in my service to the community, as I was able to help out with the recent flare-ups between Hindus and Muslims last year.

My passion for both my community and my job in the police is very important, as is being a citizen of Leicester. Since I lost my husband to cancer, I am now heavily involved in well-being and mindfulness meetings and events. In my spare time, I do dressmaking, DIY and I love cooking!

Connect with Bhanu:

https://www.linkedin.com/in/bhanu-jadeja-mahal-40171158

Pam Case

Pam Case helps businesses worldwide to market themselves and win business through LinkedIn. She's also an inspirational speaker. Over 140 testimonials span both her roles.

Pam is often asked, "Why do you speak Hindi and Urdu?"

When a business contact eked the real reason out of her, he exclaimed that her story REALLY needed to be told since it can inspire and help many.

It's proof that reaching out across the boundaries of colour, culture and creed can promote greater understanding and tolerance and, in turn, enrich our own lives.

What happened in India is revealed in this book.

Connect with Pam:

www.linkedin.com/in/pamcasecommunications
www.facebook.com/pamela.case.5437
www.instagram.com/pam.case

Alaska Harrison

Alaska Harrison is a young queer activist, creative and entrepreneur with a passion for Black liberation and empowerment of gender, sexual and relationship minorities in addition to historically marginalised communities.

Working as a writer in television and comedy development, they grew up in South-West London, beginning their career creating their own live music events aged 13 before moving into the digital media space and producing original scripted content.

Their work has taken them around the world, from shooting documentaries (funded by the Slovenian Arts Institute) in Tel Aviv to contributing to Laci Green's *Sex Plus* book published by HarperCollins, before being selected to join the prestigious Channel 4 Production Training programme operated by ThinkBigger!, working across labels at Objective Media Group in London.

Having collaborated with an array of major companies and clients across the creative industries, Alaska is currently the story editor and writer on *Captain Zero*, the American animated series created by Cutting Edge Studios, currently in development.

In 2023, Alaska is working towards becoming a museum curator with a specialisation in decolonising history and creating equity through storytelling and community-driven projects.

In their free time, Alaska enjoys gaming, creating improvisational theatre and skating with their local roller derby team, London Rockin' Rollers.

Connect with Alaska:

www.linkedin.com/in/alaskaharrison
www.linktr.ee/alaskaharrison

Zishan Khan

Zishan Khan is a serial entrepreneur, business consultant and mindset advocate. He helps new entrepreneurs and new businesses to set up systems and smart ways of working, so they can focus on what is really important for their business, rather than worry about mundane tasks.

Zishan is also a host of a podcast called Tuesday Talks. Its purpose is to inspire others with its guests' journeys. Guests are from all backgrounds and walks of life, including coaches, entrepreneurs, healers and doctors.

Zishan is also part of Mindvalley Community, hosting local coffee meet-ups and lunch in London, meeting diverse and extraordinary community members. This creates unforgettable memories, deep conversations and inspiring relationships.

Connect with Zishan:

www.linktr.ee/iamzishanofficial
www.facebook.com/iamzishanofficial
www.instagram.com/iamzishanofficial

Dr Andrea Malam BEM

Dr Andrea Malam BEM is a multi-award-winning Leader in Diversity, a role model, and a charity/volunteer ambassador who has featured in various lifestyle magazines and books.

As Andrea Malam is both a published author and a speaker, she has it in her power to inspire others to achieve their goals with emotional support, connection and empowerment. She is the author of several books, *Anglo-Indians Abroad*, and *Saving Dreams*, and has contributed chapters to several anthologies.

As a Leader in Diversity, Andrea delivers tailored mindset strategies to open-minded individuals to positively change their perception to enable Inclusion, Diversity and Equality.

Andrea is also the proud Founder Trustee of Saving Dreams, a charity inspiring others by sharing stories and experiences, and helping people succeed at any stage of their career or business.

Connect with Andrea:

www.linkedin.com/in/dr-andrea-malam-bem-b38aa313a

www.savingdreams.org.uk

www.facebook.com/savingdreamsofficial

SAVING DREAMS

Saving Dreams

Saving Dreams was founded by Andrea Malam and is a registered charity giving communities life-changing experiences, education and donations through other non-profit organisations.

The charity works towards connecting, supporting and empowering underprivileged children and their families.

The charity's main aims are:

❖ To enable children to escape poverty with support and education.

❖ To alleviate suffering while maintaining human dignity.

All projects run by the charity are only possible due to grants, donations and volunteers.

www.savingdreams.org.uk

www.instagram.com/wearesavingdreamsofficial

www.facebook.com/savingdreamsofficial

Acknowledgements

This anthology would not be possible without the various contributors; Archna Gohil, Louise Slattery, Nirmala Bhojani, Jermaine Gregory, Dr Bijna Kotak Dasani, Kate Wilson, Emma Jones, Bhanu Jadeja-Mahal, Pam Case, Alaska Harrison, and Zishan Khan. I have learned so much from them.

I would like to thank my publishing team – Brenda Dempsey, Olivia Eisinger and Zara Thatcher – as well as my family and friends for all their support through this journey.

We are all Bias Breakers in some way.

Thank You.

Dr Andrea Malam BEM